EYEWITNESS
SOCCER

Written by

HUGH HORNBY

Photographed by

ANDY CRAWFORD

Modern soccer ball

Hand fan with
a soccer scene

DK

in association with

THE NATIONAL FOOTBALL MUSEUM

Penguin Random House

REVISED EDITION

DK DELHI
Senior Art Editor Vikas Chauhan
Project Art Editor Heena Sharma **Editor** Upamanyu Das
Senior Picture Researcher Sumedha Chopra
Managing Editor Kingshuk Ghoshal
Managing Art Aditor Govind Mittal
DTP Designers Ashok Kumar, Pawan Kumar, Deepak Mittal
Jacket Designer Juhi Sheth
Senior Jackets Coordinator Priyanka Sharma Saddi

DK LONDON
Senior Editor Carron Brown **Art Editor** Chrissy Checketts
US Senior Editor Kayla Dugger
Managing Editor Francesca Baines
Managing Art Editor Philip Letsu
Production Editor Gillian Reid
Senior Production Controller Poppy David
Senior Jackets Designer Surabhi Wadhwa-Gandhi
Jacket Design Development Manager Sophia MTT
Publisher Andrew Macintyre **Associate Publishing Director** Liz Wheeler
Art Director Karen Self **Publishing Director** Jonathan Metcalf

Consultant Tracey Bourne **Authenticity Reader** Chimaoge Itabor
The National Football Museum Curators Dr. Peter Holme, Dr. Alexander Jackson

FIRST EDITION
Project Editor Louise Pritchard **Art Editor** Jill Plank
Assistant Editor Annabel Blackledge **Assistant Art Editor** Yolanda Belton
Managing Art Editor Sue Grabham
Senior Managing Art Editor Julia Harris
Production Kate Oliver **Picture Research** Amanda Russell
DTP Designers Andrew O'Brien and Georgia Bryer

This Eyewitness Book® has been conceived by
Dorling Kindersley Limited and Editions Gallimard

This American Edition, 2023
First American Edition, 2000
Published in the United States by DK Publishing
1745 Broadway, 20th Floor, New York, NY 10019

A catalog record for this book is available
from the Library of Congress.
ISBN 978-0-7440-7989-0 (Paperback)
ISBN 978-0-7440-7990-6 (ALB)

DK books are available at special discounts when
purchased in bulk for sales promotions, premiums,
fund-raising, or educational use. For details, contact:
DK Publishing Special Markets,
1745 Broadway, 20th Floor, New York, NY 10019
SpecialSales@dk.com

Printed and bound in China

For the curious
www.dk.com

MIX
Paper | Supporting
responsible forestry
FSC™ C018179

This book was made with Forest
Stewardship Council™ certified
paper—one small step in DK's
commitment to a sustainable future.
**For more information go to
www.dk.com/our-green-pledge**

1900s figure
of a female
soccer player

Official
access
badges

19th-century
girls' cleats

Wheelchair soccer

Team formation

Official FIFA
badges

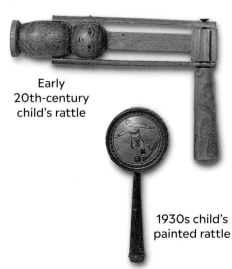

Early
20th-century
child's rattle

1930s child's
painted rattle

E Y E W I T N E S S
SOCCER

FIFA Club World Cup trophy

Early FIFA logo

1950s soccer cleat

Chocolate mold in the shape of a soccer player

Bronze statue of Benfica soccer club's eagle mascot

Leah Williamson

Contents

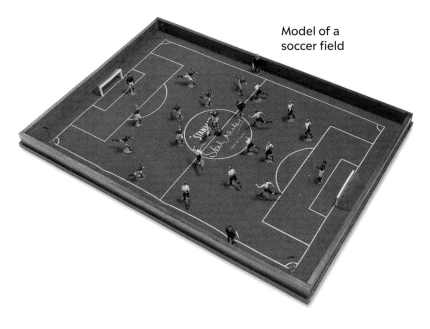

Model of a soccer field

The global game

Soccer has its roots in ancient China, Europe, and the Americas. People kicked a ball to prepare for war, to honor their gods, or just to entertain themselves. In Europe, ball-kicking games were tests of courage, while in China, they were rituals of grace and skill. The rules of the modern game of soccer were established in 1863.

Ashbourne ball

Ashbourne in Derbyshire, England, holds a traditional Shrove Tuesday soccer game. The Upwards and the Downwards teams try to move the ball through the opposition's "goal"— a gateway at the end of town.

Soccer training

The Chinese were playing a type of soccer by the 3rd century BCE. A military book of that period refers to *tsu chu*, or "kicking a ball." The game may once have been part of a soldier's training and was later included in ceremonies on the emperor's birthday.

Chinese characters meaning "soccer"

Harrow ball

English boarding schools, including Harrow and Eton, played a crucial role in developing modern soccer in the early 19th century. Although each school played the game differently, they all produced detailed written rules. These provided the basis for the first official laws.

A gentlemen's game

The game of calcio was played in Italian cities in the 16th and 17th centuries. On festival days, two teams would attempt to force the ball through openings at either end of a city square. Team tactics included formations and the creation of space in which to advance.

Handling the ball was part of the game of calcio.

Local people came out to watch the games.

Ball made from strips of leather

Players wear an elaborate costume of silk and gold brocade.

Street games

This early 19th-century cartoon is subtitled "Dustmen, coalmen, gentlemen, and city clerks at murderous if democratic play." It shows the violent "every man for himself" spirit common to street games in Britain at that time.

Ancient ritual

The Japanese game of *kemari* probably developed in the 7th century from an ancient Chinese soccer game, after contact was made between the two countries. Unlike the chaotic early soccer brawls of Europe, it involved many rituals and was played as part of a ceremony. The game is still played by keeping a ball in the air inside a small court.

Kemari is a game of balance and skill.

Color prints appear throughout the book.

16th-century discourse on soccer

18th-century anthology

The children's book *The School Across the Road*

Soccer writing

Soccer has been a literary subject for as long as the game has been played. The first book on soccer is *Discourse on Calcio* by Italian Giovanni da Bardi, published in 1580. As soccer became popular in the early 20th century, many children's books were published, including *The School Across the Road* by Desmond Coke.

History of **soccer**

The global game was developed in England and Scotland in the 19th century. Former pupils of English boarding schools produced the first common set of rules and formed the Football Association (FA) in 1863. British merchants and engineers took the game overseas, so people from other countries began to play soccer.

Exhibitionism

In the early 20th century, British teams toured the world, introducing soccer to other nations by playing exhibition matches. This shield was presented to the Islington Corinthians in Japan, in 1937.

Celebrity player

The first players were amateurs. C. B. Fry, who played for the Corinthians in the 1890s, was one of the first soccer celebrities. He also held the world long-jump record.

Arnold Kirke Smith's cap

The English Three Lions crest was first used in 1872.

Kinnaird played in nine of the first 12 FA Cup finals.

Modern rules

Lord Kinnaird was president of the Football Association from 1890 to 1923 and was one of the amateurs who shaped the rules of the modern game.

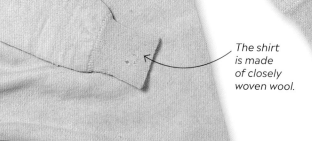

The shirt is made of closely woven wool.

Arnold Kirke Smith's England shirt

EYEWITNESS

Arthur Wharton

After moving to England from Ghana in 1883, Arthur Wharton played as an amateur soccer player at various clubs, including Preston North End. In 1889, he signed a contract with Rotherham Town FC, making him the world's first Black professional soccer player.

The first international

In November 1872, Scotland played England on a cricket field in Glasgow in the first-ever international match. About 2,000 spectators watched a 0–0 draw. This shirt and cap were worn by Arnold Kirke Smith from Oxford University, who was a member of the English team.

Out of Africa

Soccer spread through Africa. South Africa, with its European populations, sent a touring party to South America in 1906. In 1923, Egypt became the first African country to join FIFA. In 2010, South Africa became the first African country to host the World Cup finals.

Talented teams

The English Football League began in 1888. Its 12-team fixture program was inspired by baseball. This 1893 painting by Thomas Hemy shows Aston Villa and Sunderland.

The unruly game

The first French soccer league, set up in 1894, was dominated by teams of Scottish emigrants, such as the White Rovers and Standard AC. French satirists were quick to refer to the game's reputation for unruliness. This 20th century French magazine, *Le Monde Comique*, reflects this attitude toward the game.

Cover illustration entitled *"Les Plaisirs du Dimanche"* ("Sunday Pleasures")

Ladies first

Women's soccer started at the end of the 19th century. Teams such as the British Ladies Club attracted large crowds. During World War I, men's and women's teams played against each other for charity. The first Women's World Cup was held in China in 1991 and was won by the United States.

A ball of exaggerated size

FIFA badge

Forming FIFA

By 1904, many European countries had their own administrators. They formed the world governing body, FIFA (Fédération Internationale de Football Association). Today, it has more than 200 members.

US stamps produced for the 1994 World Cup

Soccer

Soccer is a popular youth sport in the United States. The 1994 World Cup finals in the US provided a boost for Major League Soccer, which is bringing professional games to a new audience.

9

Laws of the game

Soccer's success is partly due to its simple laws. Rules governing foul play, equipment, and restarts have survived the test of time. Stoppages in the game can be avoided if the referee uses the advantage rule, allowing play to continue after a foul if the right team has the ball. For the offside rule, the assistant referees decide if an attacker has strayed beyond the second-to-last defender when the ball is played forward by a teammate.

Stand back

This throw-in is illegal. The ball is held correctly in both hands, but the feet are over the line.

Before the crossbar was introduced, tape was stretched between the goal posts.

Goal kicks must be taken from within the 6-yd (5.5-m) box.

The penalty spot is 12 yd (11 m) from the goal line.

Penalty

In 1891, penalties were introduced to punish foul play, such as tripping, pushing, or a handball within 12 yd (11 m) of the goal. A player shoots from the penalty spot to beat the keeper. If the ball hits the post or bar, the penalty-taker cannot play it until another player touches it.

Free kick

There are two types of free kicks: direct and indirect. In an indirect free kick, awarded after an infringement of a law, the ball must be touched by two players before a goal is scored. Direct free kicks are given after fouls and the taker may score immediately.

Corner

A corner kick is taken when the defending team puts the ball out of play behind their own goal line. Corner kicks are good goal-scoring opportunities. The ball is placed within the quadrant—a quarter circle with a radius of 1 yd (1 m) in the corner of the field.

Faking fouls

Unlike soccer in the 19th century, the modern game has many deliberate fouls. Today's soccer players often perform a "professional foul"—a deliberate offense to prevent an attack or goal-scoring opportunity. Some players fake being fouled, or "dive" (below), to win a free kick.

To reach a maximum distance, **throw a ball** at an angle of **30 degrees**.

Law and order
There are 17 main soccer laws. The field of play must be rectangular and, for a full-size field, from 110 to 120 yd (100.5 to 110 m) long and from 70 to 80 yd (64 to 73 m) wide. There should be 11 players per side. The duration of play is 90 minutes, in two halves of 45 minutes each.

When a penalty is taken, only the taker is allowed inside the "D."

Players must not cross the halfway line until the ball is kicked off.

Players from the defending team must stay out of the 10-yd (9-m) circle before kickoff.

Assistant referees patrol opposite sides of the field and cover one half each to signal throw-ins and flag for fouls and offside (when a player is closer to the opponent's goal-line than the ball and the second-to-last defender).

Players cannot be offside on their own half of the field.

Goal nets, patented by Brodies of Liverpool, England, in 1891, were first used in 1892 to settle disputes over whether a ball had entered the goal.

Charge!
The 1958 English FA Cup final between Manchester United and Bolton Wanderers featured a disputed goal by Bolton's Nat Lofthouse. He charged United goalkeeper Harry Gregg over the line as he caught the ball. Referees would now call it a foul.

Permanent markers
In the mid-19th century, before lines were marked on the field, flags were used to decide whether the ball was out of play. Today, a corner flag has to be at least 5 ft (1.5 m) high to avoid the risk of players being impaled.

The referee

Early amateur players wanted officials to encourage fair play. Each team had an umpire. Players had to raise an arm and appeal against a foul; otherwise, play continued. The rise of professional soccer in the 1880s made it harder for umpires to be neutral. A referee was introduced to settle disputes. In 1891, the referee moved onto the field and the umpires became linesmen. They are now officially known as assistant referees.

Your number's up

The assistant referee controls the entrance of substitutes to the field and checks their cleat studs. At top levels, a fourth official uses an illuminated board to indicate the shirt numbers of the substitute and the player being replaced.

Classic black

This is the classic referee's uniform—all black with white cuffs and collar. This uniform is from the 1970s and is similar to all those worn between the phasing out of the blazer in the 1940s and the introduction of other colors in the 1990s. The bulky jackets of the early 20th century were replaced by less-constricting shirts to encourage the officials to keep up with play on the field. Modern referees may wear either a black uniform or brighter colors for better visibility on the field.

A white trim sets off the all-black uniform.

The badge refers to the referee's local association.

Referees must be smartly dressed, with shirt tucked in at all times.

Referees must wear shorts, usually black.

Notebook to record bookings, goals, sendings-off, and substitutions

The yellow card is shown for bookable offenses.

Serious foul play results in a red card and a sending-off.

1940s Acme whistle

Both sides of a FIFA Fair Play coin

Tools of the trade

Some items are vital to the referee's job. Red and yellow cards were first used at the 1970 World Cup. It is believed the whistle was first used in 1878 and became the best way to control play. The referee carries a notebook and pencil to record match details and a special coin that is tossed to decide which team kicks off in which direction.

You're booked

Bookings used to be given only once or twice a match and sendings-off were rare, but FIFA now insists that referees are strict. As a result, teams have to play with 10 team members, or even fewer.

Referees have to be fit to keep up with play on the field.

Official FIFA badges for sewing on the officials' shirts

Touchline helpers

The first linesmen waved a handkerchief to alert the referee. Assistant referees now wave a flag for when the ball is out of play, for offsides, or for any infringement of the rules.

Video assistant referee (VAR)

In 2018, the VAR (video assistant referee) was introduced by FIFA to support match officials on the field. A VAR monitors the full match, but will only contact the referee if they have made clear and obvious errors in decisions or missed serious incidents, such as goals, penalties, offsides, and direct red cards.

👁 EYEWITNESS

Pierluigi Collina
Widely regarded as the greatest referee in soccer history, Pierluigi Collina (b.1960) was known for his no-nonsense reputation. He won FIFA's Referee of the Year award six times between 1998 and 2003. In his 28-year career, Collina refereed matches in the Serie A, the FIFA Men's World Cup, and the finals of the Men's Champions League and UEFA Cup.

Slopes and shade

Most top clubs use grow lights that help the grass grow uniformly and keep the field in top condition, even in shaded areas. Modern fields, such as Brighton and Hove Albion's (shown here), are usually laid with a camber, which means they slope slightly down from the center circle to the touchlines to drain water away.

The field

At most soccer clubs, the field is smooth and green. Ground staff at clubs and national stadiums keep fields in top condition with new species of grass and good drainage. In the past, fields sometimes became muddy or froze during bad weather, but modern hybrid fields avoid this by featuring undersoil heating and efficient drainage.

Hot stuff

In colder countries, various methods have been tried to prevent soccer fields from freezing. Undersoil heating was first installed at Everton, England, in 1958. In the past, ground staff put straw down as insulation and lit fires in braziers to increase the air temperature.

Ground staff preparing for a match during the 1953 English season

Playing in snow

In snow, the ball and field markings are hard to see and the ground is slippery. If the markings are swept clear and the field is soft for studs, play can carry on. During winter, most soccer leagues use a ball with a bright color, such as orange, for better visibility in snow and rain.

Jean-Pierre Papin playing for AC Milan, Italy, on a snowy field

 EYEWITNESS

Katie Croft

Katie was one of the first female groundspeople to be employed at an English Premier League club. In 2015, at only 19 years old, she was responsible for looking after fields and playing surfaces across Manchester City's facilities, including their Academy complex.

The **stripes** on a soccer field are created by **bending** the grass in **different directions**.

Pampering the field

Modern field maintenance is a full-time job. In summer, the grass is mowed, watered, and fed regularly. During the off-season, work is done to repair holes and worn patches in the turf. Hybrid fields are restored once a year, removing old grass from between the artificial fibers and reseeding new grass.

Better than the real thing?

Artificial fields are made from synthetic turf laid on a shock-absorbent pad. They are more hard-wearing than grass fields and are unaffected by rain or ice. However, many players feel they increase the risk of injury. Today, most top clubs prefer hybrid fields, which have artificial fibers woven in with real grass to create a durable and even playing surface.

SATURATION POINT

Rainwater is the greatest threat to field condition. Built-in drainage is an important part of field construction. Pipes and materials chosen for their draining qualities are laid under grass. Lots of sand is mixed into the topsoil to make it less absorbent and less waterlogged. Even a well-cared-for field may become saturated.

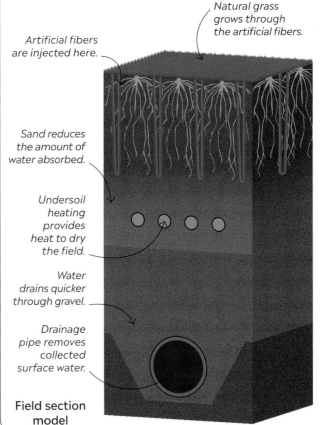

Natural grass grows through the artificial fibers.

Artificial fibers are injected here.

Sand reduces the amount of water absorbed.

Undersoil heating provides heat to dry the field.

Water drains quicker through gravel.

Drainage pipe removes collected surface water.

Field section model

Soccer skills

Each position on the field is associated with specific tasks. Defenders must tackle opponents to claim the ball, midfielders must pass the ball accurately to their teammates, and strikers must shoot and score goals. Professional players master and perfect a range of techniques and skills.

Early 20th-century button showing a man heading the ball

Heads up!

Headers can be defensive or attacking. Defenders try to gain distance when they clear a ball from the goal area. Attackers need power and accuracy to head in a goal. Kylie Ledbrook of Sydney FC (left) leaps into the air to beat Aivi Luik of Brisbane Roar (right) and head the ball. Recent studies have shown that excessive heading of the ball may cause damage to the brain and lead to medical conditions such as early onset dementia.

The player must time their leap to meet the ball firmly.

Tackle talk

Players try to take the ball from another player by tackling. French player N'golo Kante, playing here for Chelsea (in dark blue), is one of the finest tacklers in modern soccer. Anticipation and timing are essential to avoid committing a foul. Referees punish players if they make a physical challenge from behind or if they make contact with a player instead of the ball.

Pass mark

A quick play between players stretches a defense. Accurate passing is the hallmark of all successful teams. The ability to pass with both feet gives the player more options. Former Barcelona player Xavi (right) could pass the ball into space even when he was tightly marked.

All parts of the foot are used to manipulate the ball in the desired direction.

Accurate control of the ball gives players time to make good decisions, and it is vital for keeping the ball away from opponents.

Control freak

The best players always bring the ball under control. For high passes, they keep their eye on the ball and use their chest, head, thighs, or—like João Cancelo here—the top of their foot to contain the ball.

Going for goal

When shooting, players need the accuracy to find the corner of the net as well as the power to blast the ball past the goalkeeper. Edinson Cavani (in blue) of Uruguay is one of the most reliable goal scorers in world soccer.

Downtown dribbler

When a player runs with the ball at their feet, it is called dribbling. Retired Brazilian star Ronaldinho (right), who learned his soccer on the streets of Porto Alegre, would dribble the ball around his opponents. Good balance can help a dribbler change direction quickly and avoid tackles.

Winging it

Crosses, or passes in from the wings, are one way to create goal-scoring opportunities. Players who can cross the ball with pace and accuracy are valuable to a team. England and Liverpool's fullback Trent Alexander-Arnold is one of the world's best crossers.

Bicycle kick

The bicycle kick was first demonstrated in the 1930s by Brazilian forward Leônidas. With their back to the goal, players leap into the air and kick the ball as it flies over their body, while falling backward. This tactic can often catch the goalkeeper by surprise. Seen above is former Manchester United player Wayne Rooney scoring a spectacular bicycle-kick goal against their local rivals Manchester City.

Goalkeepers

As the last line of defense, a goalkeeper knows that a single mistake can cost their team a victory. Goalkeeping involves different skills. The necessity of having both a physical presence and great agility means that they have to train as hard as other players, but the reward can be a much longer career. For goalkeepers, though, there can be periods of time in which they do not touch the ball.

Clothes

Until 1909, goalkeepers were distinguishable only by their cap, making it difficult for the referee to judge who, in a goal-line scramble, was handling the ball. From 1909 to the early 1990s, they wore a shirt of a single plain color that was different from the shirts worn by the rest of their team. A rule was made forbidding short sleeves, which has now been relaxed.

Eire shirt
This yellow shirt was worn by Alan Kelly for the Republic of Ireland. He made 47 appearances, between 1957 and 1973.

The shamrock is a symbol of Ireland.

Throwing out
This painted button from the 20th century shows the keeper quickly throwing out the ball. This can be an effective way to launch an attack.

Keepers' colors
Patterns in soccer shirts have traditionally been limited to stripes and hoops, but since the rules on goalkeepers' clothes were relaxed, every combination of colors seems to have been tried. Not all of them have been easy on the eye, although fluorescent designs or bright colors are easy for defenders to see.

Goal kick
When the ball is put out behind the goal line by an attacker, the opposing team is awarded a goal kick. The goalkeeper or a defender takes the kick from inside the 6-yard (5.5-m) box.

Goalie's gloves
Until the 1970s, cotton gloves were worn only when it was wet. Modern keepers always wear gloves, which are made of a mix of flexible and supportive materials. Various coatings and pads are used to increase the gloves' grip.

Some gloves feature small protrusions that increase the area of contact with the ball and allow the keeper to punch it with more power.

A shot straight at the keeper's midriff is generally the easiest to save.

Good save

This 1950 comic cover shows that goalkeepers are often involved in spectacular action—while making a simple save or flying through the air to tip the ball away. Modern players can make the ball swerve suddenly, so keepers must keep their bodies in line with the ball. When an attacker approaches the goal with the ball, the keeper should leave their line and move toward the ball. This action, called "narrowing of the angle," reduces the target area for the attacker.

The ball should be punched out toward the wing.

Catch it

Punching the ball away from the danger area has always been popular among European and South American goalkeepers. The keeper on this 1900 book cover is trying to punch the ball clear. Modern referees rarely allow keepers to be challenged when they are trying to catch the ball.

Loud and clear

Édouard Mendy, the goalkeeper for the Senegal national team and Chelsea Football Club, controls his penalty area by shouting instructions to his teammates. This loud communication ensures that defenders line up in the best way to create a wall for a free kick and organize themselves effectively to prevent attacks from open play.

Tactics

Coaches and managers outwit the opposition by keeping their tactics secret until the match. Since soccer began, teams have lined up in different formations. Early players had the skills needed for a particular position on the field. The pace of today's game demands that players adapt to play in almost any position.

Under manager Pep Guardiola, Spanish club Barcelona won six trophies in a year using a 4-3-3 formation.

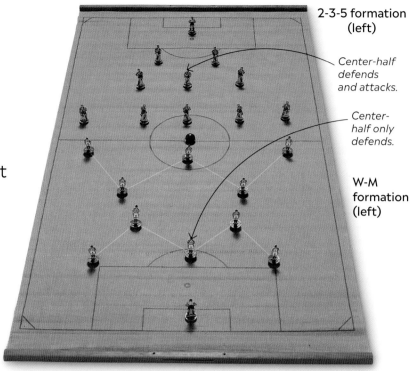

2-3-5 formation (left)

Center-half defends and attacks.

Center-half only defends.

W-M formation (left)

In good form

The 2-3-5 formation dominated tactics until the 1930s. Each player had a specific place on the field. Herbert Chapman of Arsenal, England, was the first manager to use the tactic of four lines of players set out in a 3-2-2-3 formation, creating a W shape and an M shape.

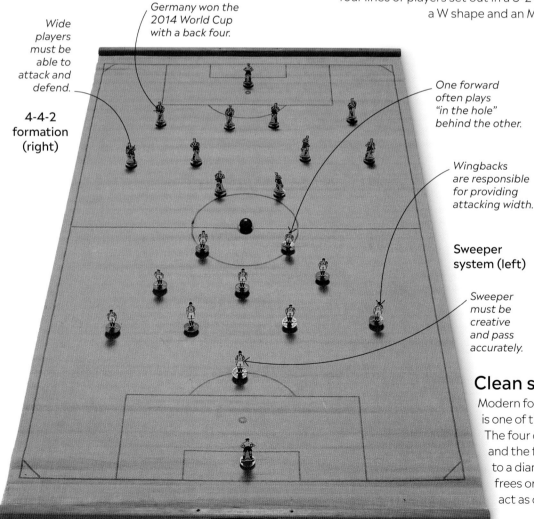

Wide players must be able to attack and defend.

Germany won the 2014 World Cup with a back four.

4-4-2 formation (right)

One forward often plays "in the hole" behind the other.

Wingbacks are responsible for providing attacking width.

Sweeper system (left)

Sweeper must be creative and pass accurately.

Game plan

Software companies have created computer programs to enable managers to plan their tactics on-screen. This 4-3-3 formation is now one of the most common in soccer. Another common one is 3-4-3.

Clean sweep

Modern formations are varied, but the 4-4-2 is one of the most used formations in history. The four defenders do not push forward and the four midfielders sometimes switch to a diamond shape. The sweeper system frees one player from marking duties to act as cover.

Packed defense

Denying the opposition forward space is vital, and certain players may be singled out for player-to-player marking. It is said that the best teams are built from the back, with a strong defense providing a springboard for attack. Here, Paris FC defenders are surrounding a striker.

The attacker is trapped.

The defenders are physically blocking in the attacker.

The forward cannot go "one on one" with the goalkeeper or the last defender unless they are in possession of the ball.

Offside origins

The first offside law, in 1866, stated that three defenders, including the goalkeeper, had to be between the attacker and the goal (above) when the ball was played forward by a teammate. By 1920, fewer goals went in because attackers still had to beat the last outfield defender.

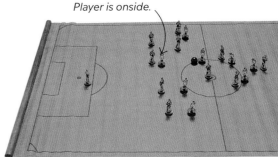

Player is onside.

Offside updated

In 1925, FIFA amended the offside law so that only two players had to be between the attacker and the goal. Far more goals were scored. The offside rule is basically unchanged today. As seen above, the midfielder is about to pass the ball to the forward. This player is still onside and will have only the goalkeeper to beat.

No substitute

FIFA introduced substitutions in 1923 if a player was injured. Injuries were faked to let coaches make tactical changes, so it was accepted that one player could be freely replaced. In 2022, the number of substitutions allowed in a match was changed from three per team to five per team.

Player is offside.

Offside trap

Teams without a sweeper can still use an offside trap. As the midfielder goes to pass the ball forward, the defenders advance up the field in a line, leaving the forward offside when the ball is played.

Injury time

A professional soccer player's job involves far more than playing matches. Training, fitness, and recovery from injuries are concerns for the modern player. Advances in medicine and technology mean more injuries can now be successfully treated. Physiotherapy, nutrition, and even psychology are all part of the routine at big clubs today.

The physiotherapist usually carries their equipment onto the field in a bag.

4 - CAMPIONATI MONDIALI DI CALCIO

NOVO: il brodo ricco di 12 saporiti ingredienti

Riproduzione vietata
Spiegazione a tergo

Vital edge

Manager Vittorio Pozzo led Italy to victory in the World Cup in 1934 and 1938. He rated physical fitness and trained his team hard to give them more stamina. This paid off in extra time in the 1934 final against Czechoslovakia when Italy scored the winner.

The "basket" shape prevents a player from sliding off the stretcher, making it more stable for players being carried off.

Crutches and neck braces can support a player with leg, neck, or head injuries.

Patient safety straps secure the player in the stretcher and stop the body moving, preventing further injury.

Fighting fit

Heavy medicine balls like this were used in soccer training for many decades to build muscle bulk and improve stamina. Gym equipment, training programs, and resistance machines are now commonly used. Strength and fitness are essential to success because top players have to play as many as 70 games per season.

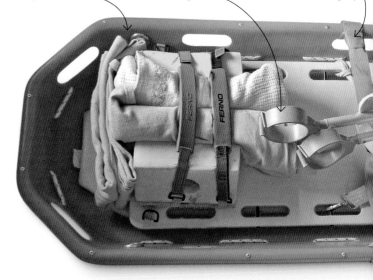

Receiving treatment

Former West Bromwich Albion player Stéphane Sessègnon is treated by physiotherapists for an ankle injury during a Premier League match. Physiotherapists are fully qualified to give sophisticated treatment to injured players both on and off the field. Sometimes doctors may need to be around to deal with serious issues. Due to an increase in heart-related incidents over the years, a team's doctors stay ready on the sidelines with defibrillators and other emergency medical equipment.

Up and down

Modern players know the importance of warming up before a game. The risk of muscle tears and strains is significantly reduced if the muscles are warm and loose. Many teams "cool down" after a match to relax their muscles before resting them.

As if by magic

The "magic" spray has a special place in soccer folklore. Spectators have often wondered how a mysterious spray could result in a player's swift recovery from an injury. Most sprays contain ingredients that help cool down an affected area and reduce muscle swelling, or chemicals that temporarily numb the pain so that a player is able to play through the remainder of the match.

Getting carried away

In the 1920s, if a stretcher was brought out onto the field, the crowd knew that a player was seriously injured. Today, players who are injured have to leave the field after treatment, and if fit to resume, are only allowed to rejoin play a few moments later. Modern stretchers have the latest equipment to treat and support an injured player. In many countries, motorized carts have taken the place of traditional stretchers.

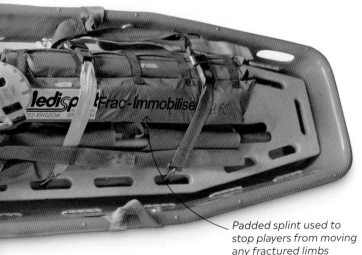

Padded splint used to stop players from moving any fractured limbs

EYEWITNESS

Fabrice Muamba
English midfielder Fabrice Muamba (b.1988) played for Arsenal, Birmingham City, and Bolton Wanderers. During an FA Cup match in 2012, he suffered a cardiac arrest, during which his heart stopped for 78 minutes. He recovered, but had to retire from playing. He later became a youth coach.

Soccer balls

The game of soccer can be played without any special equipment. Children can kick around a tennis ball or a rubber-band ball. Centuries ago, people found that an animal's bladder could be inflated and knotted to make a light, bouncy ball. A bladder did not last long when kicked, so people protected bladders in a shell of animal skin cured to turn it into leather. This design is still used today but with modern, synthetic materials.

Orange soccer balls were once used in
snowy conditions
so that players could see the ball.

Full of air

Over time, air escaped from a soccer ball's bladder and a pump was used to reinflate it. Air pressure in a bladder could be increased to improve the bounce. If a bladder was pumped too high, it could burst, so some pumps came with their own pressure gauge.

The handle is pushed down to the cylinder to pump up the bladder.

The Nesthill brass pump

The sykometer measures air pressure.

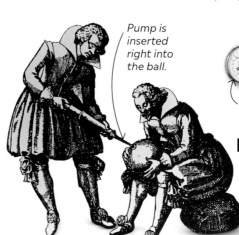

Pump is inserted right into the ball.

Ball boys

This 17th-century German engraving shows that inflated animal bladders have been used for a long time.

Sections of leather are sewn together.

An 1890s brass traveling inkwell in the shape of a soccer ball

Tool for lacing the ball tightly

Heavy going

Balls of the 1870s were often formed by stitching together eight segments of leather, the ends of which were secured by a central disk. The leather was unprotected and could absorb water on wet days, so the ball increased in weight. Heading the ball could be dangerous, so this technique was not often used in those days. The dribbling game was popular, and the heavy ball was suitable for this style of play.

Made to measure

This ball was used in March 1912 in a match between Wales and England. Made from a rubber bladder wrapped in leather, it is typical of the balls used for most of the 20th century. The outside shell was laced up. The size and weight of soccer balls were standardized for the first FA Challenge Cup competition in 1872, but the balls still absorbed water and lost shape.

Alternative balls

Several different soccer games are played around the world. They each use a ball specific to that game. Some soccer games have existed for centuries. The balls may have features connected to a ceremonial aspect of the game and involve decoration, or they are designed to withstand very harsh treatment.

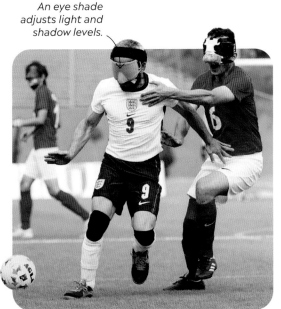

An eye shade adjusts light and shadow levels.

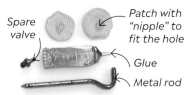

Spare valve

Patch with "nipple" to fit the hole

Glue

Metal rod

Patching things up

This 1970s repair kit was used with a vinyl ball. The metal rod was heated and inserted into the puncture to create a hole, onto which a patch could be glued.

Blind soccer

Blind soccer is an adapted version of five-a-side futsal (a five-a-side soccer game played on a hard indoor court). This sport can be played by disabled players who are blind or have partially impaired vision, although the goalkeepers are usually sighted. The soccer ball contains ball bearings that create noise when it rolls across the ground so that the players can hear it moving.

Wheelchair soccer

Wheelchair soccer is a fast-moving 4-v-4 game, which can be played by disabled players who use an electric or manual wheelchair. It is played indoors and with a size 9 soccer ball, 12.9 in (33 cm) in diameter, to match the size of the chairs.

Interlocking panels of leather

Laces for tightening the case

Manufacturers' names were first stenciled on balls in about 1900.

The brand name is marked on the ball with a stencil.

The colors are based on the French flag.

Heading for trouble

Balls such as this one were used at the 1966 World Cup when the design had hardly changed in 50 years. The leather case was lined—a 1940s development to improve durability. The outside was painted with a pigment and rubbed with wax to repel water from a rain-soaked field. Manufacturers had not found an alternative to lacing up the ball, so players risked injury when heading the ball.

World Cup colors

The first World Cup balls to have a color other than black and white printed on them were used at the 1998 World Cup in France. They had a synthetic coating to make them waterproof and a foam layer between the latex bladder and polyester skin. This let players pass and shoot quickly. These balls were made in the Sialkot region of Pakistan.

Cleats

Of all soccer equipment, cleats have changed the most in the last 100 years. The fast sport we see today would be impossible if soccer players had to use the heavy, painful cleats worn until the 1930s. In the first World Cup tournaments in the 1930s, South American teams wore lighter low-cut cleats, starting the trend toward the modern, high-tech cleat. Today, many companies sponsor players to raise the profile and boost the sales of their brand of cleats.

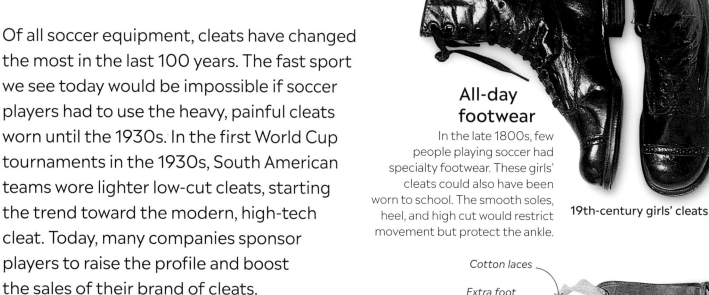

All-day footwear

In the late 1800s, few people playing soccer had specialty footwear. These girls' cleats could also have been worn to school. The smooth soles, heel, and high cut would restrict movement but protect the ankle.

19th-century girls' cleats

Studless cleats

A 19th-century gentleman soccer player wore studless cleats, which would not have allowed for sharp turns or long passing. However, they were practical enough for the type of dribbling game favored by many English amateur teams.

Cleats like these would get much heavier when wet.

Cotton laces

Extra foot support

Cleats in the bathtub

In 1910, these cleats were marketed as "Cup Final Specials," an early example of a soccer product being tied to a famous match. The wickerwork pattern on the toes was meant to help ball control. It was common for players to wear new cleats in the bathtub to soften the leather.

Sponsorship deals

Over the last 50 years, star players have received huge sums of money to wear popular brands of soccer cleats. In 2020, Brazilian superstar Neymar signed a world-record deal with German sportswear company Puma, which would see him earn around $26 million every year for wearing their cleats.

Lots of laces

Paton's cleat laces, in various colors, were widely used from the 1930s onward. There was a constant demand for replacements because repeated soaking during matches, followed by drying out, caused the early cotton laces to perish and eventually snap.

STUDS AND STUFF

The number and the position of studs on the sole varies greatly. Longer studs are needed for a wet and muddy field, while shorter ones are worn on a hard field. Modern cleats often feature studs of a fixed length molded to the sole of the cleat. The risk of studs causing injury concerns the game's governing bodies. The referee or an assistant must check the studs of everyone entering the field of play.

Wooden hammer

The first studs
Early soccer cleats were made entirely of leather. The studs had to be hammered into the soles.

Harmful hammers
Rubber studs came next. They also needed nailing to the sole, and it was not long before the cleats were damaged.

All change!
Modern screw-in studs are made of plastic or metal. Players can change studs at halftime.

These high-cut cleats offered a good amount of ankle protection.

England's Tom Finney promoted these cleats.

A "kick around" is a popular pastime with children.

The modern look
The classic black-with-white-trim design became popular in the 1950s. The cleats were flexible enough to be worn without much breaking-in. There was less protection around the ankle, which allowed players to move freely but led to an increase in injuries.

Made for the job
By the 1920s, soccer cleats like the "Manfield Hotspur" were being mass-produced for soccer players of all ages. Children's cleats were designed just like adults', with reinforced toecaps and heels and leather studs. Social conditions at the time meant that most working-class families could not afford such equipment.

The designer age
Huge sums of money are spent on the development of modern cleats. Top-quality leather uppers and light synthetic soles combine to make cleats that last. They are comfortable and allow amazing amounts of spin on the ball. Many players wear customized cleats that feature unique designs such as their personal branding or images of popular animated characters.

Soccer uniform

A shirt, shorts, and socks form the basis of a soccer player's outfit. Players in hotter countries needed cool clothing, so over time, wool gave way to cotton and then artificial fibers. Cool fabrics that "breathe" are now the norm worldwide. Teams wear matching outfits on the field of play in the club colors, which all the fans can identify. Women's teams started wearing soccer outfits in the early 1900s. Today, they wear uniforms customized for them.

In the 19th century, both soccer and rugby players wore knee-length knickerbockers with no leg protection.

Wool sweaters

In the late 19th century, soccer jerseys were often made from wool. They stretched out of shape and became heavy during rain.

Lace-ups

At all levels of the game, teams began to wear matching colors. This black-and-white shirt was worn by a Newcastle United player at the 1911 English FA Cup final. Newcastle still wear black and white today. The shirt is made of thick cotton with a lace-up collar.

Australian amateurs

This wool Australian shirt with a cotton collar was worn in 1925 by Tommy Traynor. Shirts worn in international games have symbolic importance. After a game, teams swap shirts as a gesture of goodwill.

Dutch orange

The orange uniform of the Netherlands is instantly recognizable. Dutch fans wear replica shirts to form an orange mass at matches. Here, Dutch forward Vivianne Miedema wears the national uniform.

Away color

In the 1966 World Cup final, the England team wore red instead of their usual white home color. This was because West Germany were wearing white.

Pull your socks up

Modern socks are made from high-performance materials. Many players now wear "grip" socks (above right), which have numerous pads along the back and bottom to stop the player from slipping in their cleats when on the field. Players often cover their grip socks with sock "sleeves" (above left) that match their team's colors.

Keeping cool

Modern shirts are designed to keep players cool and draw away excess moisture. This 2018–2019 Netherlands shirt is made of light and durable synthetic fabrics that suit today's high-energy games.

Cream flannel shorts from about 1900

Modern synthetic shorts with slits at the bottom edges

Hard-wearing cotton shorts from the 1930s

Short story

Amateurs in the 1860s played in full-length pants, but as the game developed, players had to increase their speed and agility. Shorter knickerbockers cut just above the knee became popular. The baggy style of soccer shorts of the 1930s was made famous by Alex James of Arsenal, England. Modern soccer shorts are made of flexible, breathable fabric that allows a full range of movement.

Accessories

A buttoned tunic was an alternative to the more common shirt.

Reinforced guards

This figure is from the box of a late 19th-century German soccer game. His shin guards are strengthened with cane bars.

Injury and discomfort were part of soccer in its early days. This situation improved when protective equipment and other accessories such as hats and belts were introduced at the end of the 19th century. Shin guards were developed in 1874 to protect players from injuries during games. Leg protection is still part of a player's uniform, but many other accessories are no longer used.

The only players allowed to wear a cap in the modern game are **goalkeepers,** who can wear a baseball cap.

This type of shin guard was made of brown leather, and lined inside with tubed bamboo "stiffeners" for protection.

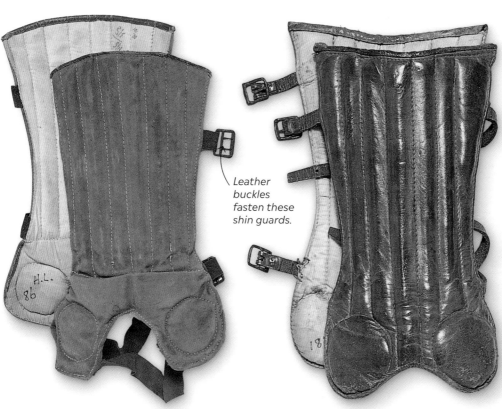

Leather buckles fasten these shin guards.

The first shin guards

The earliest shin guards, which were similar to cricket pads, were worn outside the socks and were extended to include ankle protectors, which rested on the top of the cleat. Some, such as these, had a suede covering, which was prone to water damage. These heavy and inflexible pads date from the 1890s, about 20 years after shin guards became part of the soccer player's uniform.

Lasting design

In the 1900s, players wore shin guards such as these outside their socks, held in place with straps and buckles. The front is leather, the back is cotton, and the stuffing in between is animal hair.

Room to move

By 1910, ankle protection was no longer part of shin-guard design because it restricted movement of the foot. Passing and running off the ball were now important parts of the game, requiring increased flexibility of the ankle. Players were therefore forced to sacrifice some protection.

Women's hats and belt from 1895

Early 20th-century schoolboys' belts

Hats and belts

In the 1890s, hats began to be commonly used by female soccer players to keep their hair covered. Belts were a part of many soccer uniforms until the 20th century. They smartened up appearances by holding in the shirt and often gave teams identity through the use of colors.

Keeping warm

Gloves have become common, especially among players from countries with warmer climates who play in Europe, often in freezing temperatures. Players susceptible to hamstring and groin injuries wear undershorts to keep these areas warm.

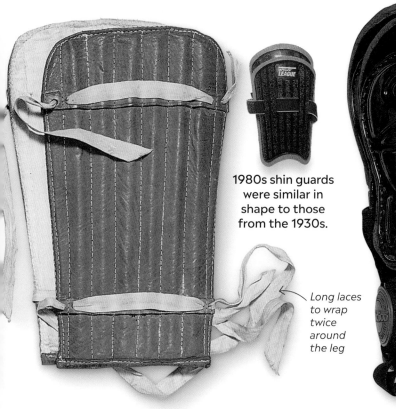

1980s shin guards were similar in shape to those from the 1930s.

Long laces to wrap twice around the leg

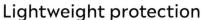

Modern shin guards can be customized, with players adding their name, number, or pictures of themselves.

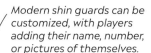

Tie-on shin guards

Shin guards worn inside the socks took over by 1930. Laces were used for fastening instead of buckles to prevent chafing on the players' legs. Many years later, tighter-fitting synthetic, rather than wool, socks held the pads firmly in place.

Lightweight protection

Shin guards from the 1990s and early 2000s looked very different from earlier models. They were shaped to fit the leg, using lightweight materials to give excellent protection. Even the delicate Achilles tendon at the back of the ankle was shielded.

Flexible and streamlined

Modern shin guards are sleek, compact, and ultra-lightweight. Most players prefer to place their shin guards in a compression sleeve, which holds them in place without restricting any form of leg or ankle movement.

Famous players

Soccer is a team game. Clubs and national sides inspire the greatest passion among fans, but a few players are so gifted and entertaining that they stand out and draw huge audiences. All of the great players share an ability to change the course of a match through a moment of incredible individual skill.

Gordon Banks (1937–2019)

English goalkeeper Gordon Banks is best known for a super save that kept out Pelé's header in the 1970 World Cup. Banks won 73 caps between 1963 and 1972.

Johann Cruyff (1947–2016)

One of the few great players to have become a successful manager, Dutch legend Johann Cruyff displayed great tactical awareness. He also personified the idea of "total soccer" by floating all over the field using balance and skill to open up defenses.

Gerd Müller (1945–2021)

Known as *"Der Bomber,"* Gerd Muller was a springy center-forward and a prolific goalscorer, with 68 goals in 62 games for West Germany. While playing club soccer for Bayern Munich, he scored a record 365 goals.

Bobby Charlton (b.1937)

Manchester United star Bobby Charlton was known for powerful and accurate shooting and proved invaluable in England's 1966 World Cup win. He was knighted in 1994.

Roger Milla (b.1952)

Two-time African Player of the Year, Cameroon's Roger Milla was one of the first African players to gain global fame. He was also the oldest player to score in a World Cup match, in 1994, at age 42.

Diego Maradona (1960–2020)

Maradona was the best player of his generation. He inspired his teammates, notably when leading Argentina to victory in the 1986 World Cup and Napoli to two Series A titles in Italy. His magical left foot and strength in possession were his main assets.

Maradona's low center of gravity gave him excellent balance.

Eusébio practices ball control in training

Eusébio scored 38 goals in 46 international games.

Eusébio (1942–2014)

Although he was born in Mozambique, Eusébio was signed by Benfica of Lisbon, Portugal, and went on to play for Portugal. He starred in the 1962 European Cup final, scoring twice as Benfica beat Real Madrid of Spain. Eusébio was respected all over the world for his fair play and dignity as well as for his soccer talent.

Giuseppe Meazza (1910–1979)

Italian Giuseppe Meazza (left) won two World Cup winner's medals, in 1934 and 1938. He was a creator and scorer of goals from his inside-forward position. In 1938, he organized the Italian team when the coach was ordered to the stands. His best years were at Internazionale of Milan, Italy.

Garrincha (1933–1983)

Nicknamed "Little Bird," Garrincha had polio as a child. He overcame his disability to become one of the quickest and most elusive wingers the game has seen. He played on the right-hand side of Brazil's legendary 1958 forward line. In 1962, he made up for the absence of the injured Pelé with some brilliant performances, helping Brazil retain the World Cup.

Continued on next page

Continued from previous page

Zinedine Zidane (b.1972)

One of the greatest players of modern times, the French attacking-midfielder Zinedine Zidane combined physical strength with skill and intelligence. In 1998, he propelled France to their first World Cup win, with two goals against Brazil in the final. He also helped Real Madrid to victory in the 2002 Champions League final with a man-of-the-match performance.

Lionel Messi (b.1987)

A skillful forward, Lionel Messi made his competitive debut for Barcelona at age 16 and has since won 10 Spanish league championships. He has also won one French league championship with Paris Saint-Germain. The Argentina captain has won the FIFA Ballon d'Or a record-breaking seven times.

Cristiano Ronaldo (b.1985)

Portugal's captain Cristiano Ronaldo is one of the world's best players. He has won the Ballon d'Or five times and scored a staggering 816 goals for club and country. Ronaldo played for Real Madrid from 2009 to 2018, during which he led the team to four UEFA Champions League victories.

Christine Sinclair (b.1983)

With 186 goals and 296 caps, Canada's Sinclair holds the record for most international goals scored by a man or a woman, and for being the most-capped international player.

Lev Yashin (1929–1990)

Always in black, Lev Yashin played for the Soviet Union in four World Cups and is the only keeper to be named European Footballer of the Year.

Franz Beckenbauer (b.1945)

Beckenbauer remains one of the few soccer legends to achieve similar success as a manager. He captained West Germany to victory at the 1974 World Cup and led them to the title as manager in 1990.

Ferenc Puskás (1927–2006)

The star of Hungary's famous team of the 1950s, Puskás joined Real Madrid of Spain in 1958. Puskás favored his left foot, scoring many goals for club and country.

Marta (b.1986)

Marta Vieira da Silva is regarded as one of the best female soccer players of all time. She has been the FIFA World Player of the Year six times and holds the record for the most goals scored in the World Cup.

Megan Rapinoe (b.1985)

Winger Megan Rapinoe led the US women's national team to two Olympic medals (in 2012 and 2021) and two World Cup victories (in 2015 and 2019). Rapinoe's soccer career reached new heights in 2019 when she won the Ballon d'Or Féminin, the FIFA Women's Player of the Year, the World Cup Golden Ball, and the World Cup Golden Boot.

Pelé (b.1940)

Many people's choice of the greatest player of all, Pelé was king of Brazilian soccer from the late 1950s to the early 1970s. He scored more than 1,000 goals for Brazilian club Santos, American soccer team New York Cosmos, and Brazil. His enthusiasm and love of soccer make him a perfect role model for the game.

Winning **feeling**

Soccer players lucky enough to win a championship are awarded a medal for their achievement. Those good enough to be picked to play for their country win a cap. Medals and caps have been part of the game since the 19th century and are still highly valued rewards today. Success can be measured by the number of caps a player has, and passing the 100-cap mark is considered exceptional service to the national team.

Badge from a 1954 England international shirt, worn in a match against Yugoslavia

Club strikers
Some clubs strike their own medals to mark a special achievement of their players. This medal was awarded to Preston North End players at the end of their title-winning 1903–1904 season.

Medals

As with military medals for soldiers, soccer players are rewarded with medals for helping their side. Medals are awarded at all levels of soccer, professional and amateur. These mementos of glory days can become valuable collectors' items.

Good sport
Before organized leagues, soccer medals were often awarded for sportsmanship. The fullback C. Duckworth was given this medal for "gentlemanly and successful play" in the 1883–1884 season.

Doublet
These medals were won by English player Bob Haworth, who played for Preston North End and in international games for the national team.

Champion
This medal was awarded to a player for success in the 1914–1915 season.

Argentine maté pot

Ornate silver dagger

England v Scotland, 1893

FA Cup 1888–1889

Arsenal
This 1930s medal may belong to Arsenal soccer star Alex James.

Amateur
This 1920s medal was given to a successful amateur player.

Norwegian silver spoon

Argentine silver spoon

Playoff prizes
Medals have been presented to the winners of the third and fourth place playoff match at every World Cup except 1950. At the 2006 World Cup, host nation Germany won third-place medals.

With compliments
This "complimentary medal for defeating all comers" was awarded in the 1884–1885 season.

Trophy triumph
This plaque marked a match between France and England in 1947. The English players received the plaque for victory.

Precious gifts
International players can receive gifts from opposing soccer associations. The England team received silver spoons from Norway in 1949. The Argentine FA gave the English team ceremonial daggers and other silverware in 1951.

War games
Throughout World War II, famous international players took part in exhibition matches arranged to boost public morale. In 1946, Tom Finney was given this medal after a match in Belgium.

Africa Cup of Nations
This medal was presented to the winners of the first Africa Cup of Nations. Sudan, Ethiopia, and Egypt took part. Egypt won the final 4–0.

In training
Trainer Will Scott received this medal when the English and Scottish Leagues met at Celtic Park, Scotland, in 1931.

Promotional medal
By the 1950s, businesses commemorated soccer events. French newspaper *Le Soir* made this medal for a 1953 club tour.

World Cup
The biggest achievement in soccer is to win the World Cup. This Jules Rimet medal is from the 1954 final, when West Germany beat the favorites, Hungary.

Home cap
This Welsh cap was awarded for the 1903–1904 Home International matches between England, Scotland, Northern Ireland, and Wales. This tournament took place every year until 1984.

Soccer caps are often made from velvet.

Tassels are added for decoration.

Welsh national crest—a dragon

Caps
A colored cap was once the only way to know which team a player was on. In 1872, the FA ruled that teams should wear distinctive shirts. In 1886, it was suggested that caps be awarded to soccer players each time they played for their country. Today, they are given to every member of a national team, including playing substitutes. Wayne Rooney was the youngest player to reach 100 caps for England and was awarded a golden cap.

Northern Ireland has had its own team since 1921.

Carey's cap
Defender Johnny Carey won this cap playing for Ireland in 1938. He won 36 caps.

School colors
Soccer caps were first awarded in English public schools. "Colors," or caps, were given to the year's best players.

Big clubs

Clubs inspire the greatest loyalty and passion from soccer fans. Big clubs in every country attract followers from around the world and usually dominate their domestic leagues and cups. Success for these clubs often continues because strong financial backing ensures a steady supply of good new players.

The Old Lady

Juventus are the most successful Italian club and enjoy great support outside Turin. Nicknamed "The Old Lady" (*La Vecchia Signora*), they won the European Cup in 1985 and 1996.

London ladies

Netty Honeyball was the force behind the first great women's team in the 1890s. The British Ladies Club drew large crowds for their exhibition matches across the UK.

Baines card from the 1890s showing a Newton Heath player named Jack Powell

PLAY UP NEWTON HEATH

POWELL

Busby babes

English club Manchester United started as Newton Heath before their name change in 1902. The Munich air disaster of 1958 killed eight members of manager Matt Busby's young team. The club have since won three European Cups.

Real rivalry

In recent years, Spanish giants Real Madrid have taken a step ahead of their fierce rivals Barcelona as the biggest team in the country. In the 2021–2022 season, Real Madrid won four major titles: La Liga, the Copa del Rey cup, the UEFA Champions League, and the UEFA Super Cup.

Bravo Benfica

Only Porto and Sporting Lisbon rival Benfica in the Portuguese League. Benfica were the great team of the early 1960s, winning two European Cups, in 1961 and 1962, and reaching but losing three further finals. This bronze depicts Benfica's symbol, an eagle.

South American icons

Boca Juniors are the most successful club in Argentina. They've won a total of 72 official titles, including 34 Argentine Primera Division championships, six Copa Libertadores, and 34 cup competitions—both domestic and international.

Bossing the league

Al-Sadd SC are a Qatari soccer club based out of Doha. They are Qatar's most successful club, having won a record 16 titles in the country's top league, the Qatar Star League. Their achievements have earned them the nickname "the boss."

Brilliant Barcelona

Spanish club Barcelona Femení is one of the best teams in women's soccer. For three years in a row, from 2020 to 2022, they won their domestic league, the Liga F. They completed their trophy-laden season as the winners of the UEFA Women's Champions League in 2022.

Young talent

In the 1970s, Dutch club Ajax's policy to develop its own young players bore fruit. The players, including Johann Cruyff, helped Ajax to three consecutive European Cup wins in the 1970s. With arguably the best academy system in the world, Ajax continue to produce world-class players, such as Frenkie De Jong and Justin Kluivert, for top European leagues.

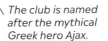

The club is named after the mythical Greek hero Ajax.

The fans

Fans have made soccer the world's biggest game. From the late 19th century, working people began to have free time to attend sporting events. They created an atmosphere of excitement and expectation. Today, soccer is the most widely watched sport in the world. Fans show their support for club and country in a range of noisy and colorful ways.

Club colors

Colors are a vital part of the bond between a team and its supporters. Fans often wear a scarf with club colors to show their loyalty, such as the yellow and blue of Turkish club Fenerbahçe seen here.

Perfect view

In their desperation to see a game, fans are not always put off by the "ground full" signs. In the 19th century, before large-scale stands were built, trees provided a convenient spot from which to watch a popular match.

Props for support

In England in the late 1980s, there was a craze for taking large inflatables to matches. Fans waved bananas, fish, and fried eggs in the crowd to show their support for their teams.

Child's piggy bank

Rare collection

Fans have always collected soccer-related objects. Today's items feature favorite clubs, but past designs were general soccer scenes. Collecting autographs or taking "selfies" is also popular and offers the opportunity to meet star players.

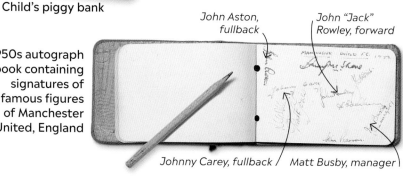

John Aston, fullback

John "Jack" Rowley, forward

1950s autograph book containing signatures of famous figures of Manchester United, England

Johnny Carey, fullback

Matt Busby, manager

Wooden pencil case showing a soccer match

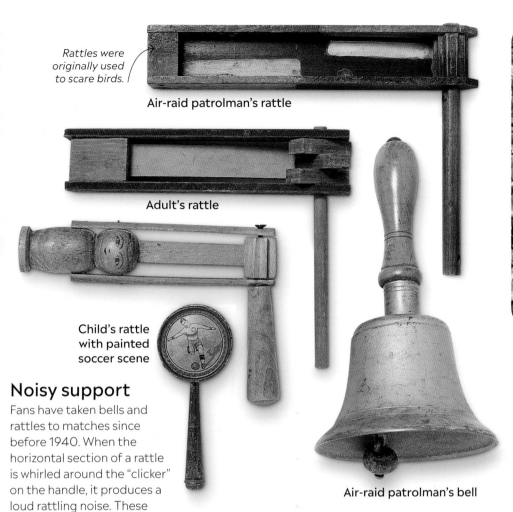

Rattles were originally used to scare birds.

Air-raid patrolman's rattle

Adult's rattle

Child's rattle with painted soccer scene

World beaters

Brazilian fans are famous for their noisy support. They produce a samba beat on the drums, which is accompanied by loud chants and whistles. As the noise echoes around the stands, fans often dance along with the beat to add to the spectacle of the game.

Noisy support

Fans have taken bells and rattles to matches since before 1940. When the horizontal section of a rattle is whirled around the "clicker" on the handle, it produces a loud rattling noise. These were part of the atmosphere at games until they were banned in the 1970s. Since the 1960s, organized chanting has been more common among fans.

Air-raid patrolman's bell

The color of the face paint may reflect the colors of the national flag or the team's jersey.

Face painting

Two Japanese fans enjoy an international friendly match between Japan and Serbia. Face-painting in team colors is common at international matches today.

Match **day**

The atmosphere of a big game, the sound of the crowd, and the closeness of the players combine to make live soccer matches so memorable. Soccer is now shown widely on television, but millions of fans still go to the matches. Many supporters are superstitious, just like the players, and follow similar match routines. Their noisy support is essential to the team's performance.

All dressed up
This photo shows fans of West Ham, England, preparing to travel to the 1923 FA Cup final, the first at Wembley. Many more than the official attendance of 123,000 crammed into the stadium.

Crowd control
Police and stewards attend soccer matches to ensure spectator safety. Law enforcement personnel, such as these officers at a Scottish Premiership match between Ross County and Motherwell, may need to control unruly fans, sometimes using horses, dogs, or riot shields to manage large crowds. They may also control traffic and escort supporters to and from the match.

Reading material
The earliest programs were simple one-sheet items, giving team line-ups. Over time, further elements were added, such as a message from the manager and background information about the opposition. Glossy, full-color brochures are now produced for all top-level matches.

Prematch excitement
Hundreds of fans of different ages gather together before a match in a "fan zone," such as these Bayern Munich fans outside the Allianz Stadium in Munich, Germany. Fan zones build excitement and anticipation before big games. Often in public areas, such as city squares, or outside a stadium, they offer food and drink stalls, entertainment, interactive activities, merchandise stalls, and big screens to watch the match on.

Major League fun

In the United States and Canada, there is a lot of fanfare at Major League Soccer (MLS) matches. Cheerleaders and music keep the crowds entertained, and teams have passionate fans. Seen above are Seattle Sounders supporters during an away game at Los Angeles Galaxy's stadium.

Official badge from 1905

FA badge from 1898

1903 FA official's badge

Badge worn at 1899 England v Scotland international

No access

Certain areas of the stadium, such as the boardroom, have strict access. These badges were sewn onto blazers worn by Football Association officials. Today, executive boxes are a feature of many grounds.

Tickets please

Tickets are essential for controlling access to games and keeping attendance to a safe level. Years ago, this was only necessary at cup finals and World Cup matches. Each match ticket corresponds to a particular seat. Today, electronic tickets are used instead of paper tickets.

Let me entertain you

To make matches more enjoyable, clubs and governing bodies put on extra entertainment before kickoff and at halftime. In the past, this often took the form of brass bands. The opening ceremony at the 2022 UEFA Champions League final in Paris, France, featured a performance by Cuban-American singer Camila Cabello.

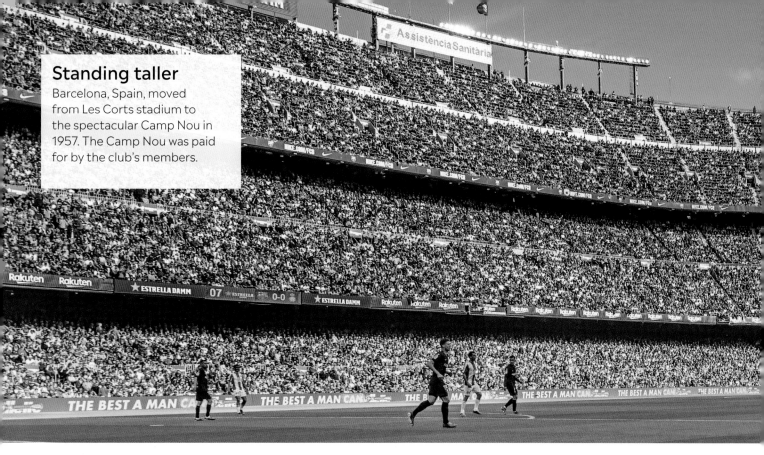

Standing taller
Barcelona, Spain, moved from Les Corts stadium to the spectacular Camp Nou in 1957. The Camp Nou was paid for by the club's members.

The stadium

As crowds grew larger in the late 19th century, soccer clubs needed somewhere permanent to hold their matches. Stadiums became a necessity, giving fans shelter and a good view. A series of stadium disasters around the world led to standing terraces being replaced by all-seater stands for the safety of spectators. Better construction and safety standards have led to the reintroduction of safe standing areas at English Premier League stadiums in 2022.

A new light
Floodlights were first used in 1878. The most common lighting was on pylons in the stadium corners. Today, floodlights often run all the way around a stadium's roof.

Fans on their feet
Before all-seater stadiums were introduced, fans stood packed on terraces. Far more fans could get in to watch a match, and it is how most people have watched games in soccer's history. Children were often passed to the front for a better view.

SHEFFIELD WEDNESDAY F.C.

Crowd safety
On 15 April 1989, at the FA Cup final at Hillsborough, Sheffield, England, 96 Liverpool fans died after a crowd crush. After the tragedy, there were new advances in stadium safety.

State of the art

When the Wembley Stadium in north London opened in 2007, the public flocked to this stunning stadium, with its 90,000 capacity and giant screens, each the size of 600 television sets. The stadium boasts a fantastic steel arch that is lit up at night and can be seen across the city.

Path to the field

The tunnel is more than just a route onto the field. It is the place where players psych themselves up for the game. Many tunnels are designed to affect the psychology of the opponents. For example, Arsenal's Emirates Stadium has life-size Arsenal players on both walls of the tunnel to intimidate their opponents.

World Cup wonder

The Luzhniki Stadium in Moscow, Russia, hosted the 2018 World Cup final between France and Croatia. The stadium's roof, enclosing the ground in a continuous curve, creates an amphitheater effect.

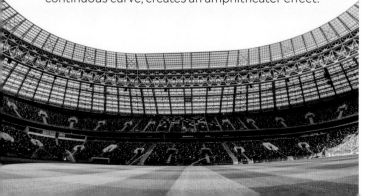

Keeping up-to-date

Modern stands are designed using computer models. Space between seats is an issue. More space means greater comfort but a reduced capacity. But many modern stadiums aim to host large audiences. The Tottenham Hotspur Stadium in London, England, can seat 62,850 spectators.

The World Cup

Soccer's World Cup is one of the greatest sporting events. The first World Cup was held in Uruguay in 1930. Some teams could not travel to the host country until the 1950s, when travel became easier and quicker. As the tournament became more accessible, it grew in popularity. In 1958, Brazilian teenager Pelé became soccer's first global superstar, and interest in the World Cup boomed.

Mascots
Every World Cup since 1966 has had a mascot. They feature as life-size figures and promotional merchandise. This is Pique, from Mexico '86.

World first
Uruguay offered to pay travel for the 13 visiting teams at the first World Cup. Four European teams made the long journey to join the South American teams.

Venues
The logo for the World Cup has changed with each event. The tournament has been held in many countries—a number of countries want to host this event to attract visitors. The 2002 finals in Japan and South Korea were the first shared tournament. Russia hosted the tournament in 2018, while Qatar hosted the 2022 edition, making it the first time the World Cup finals were played in the Middle East.

1954—Switzerland. West Germany beat Hungary 3-2 in one of the Cup's great upsets.

1958—Sweden. Brazil beat Sweden 5-2.

1962—Chile. Brazil beat Czechoslovakia 3-1, with Garrincha taking center stage.

1950—Brazil. Uruguay beat Brazil 2-1 in the first tournament after World War II.

1966—England. West Germany lost 2-4 to England, with Geoff Hurst scoring the first hat-trick in a final.

1938—France. Italy beat Hungary 4-2, inspired by inside-forward Meazza.

1970—Mexico. One of the greatest teams ever, Brazil beat Italy 4-1.

1934—Italy. Czechoslovakia lost 1-2 to Italy.

1930—Uruguay. Uruguay beat Argentina 4-2, the first of many hosts to win the Cup.

1974—West Germany. The Netherlands were beaten 2-1 by West Germany.

Mexico was the first country to host two finals.

The Italia '90 mascot was called Ciao.

1998—France. Brazil lose to France 0-3.

1978—Argentina. The Netherlands lost 1-3 to Argentina.

1982—Spain. Italy beat West Germany 3-1.

1986—Mexico. Diego Maradona's Argentina beat West Germany 3-2.

1990—Italy. West Germany beat Argentina 1-0 in a defensive final.

1994—United States. Brazil beat Italy 3-2 on penalties, winning their fourth Cup.

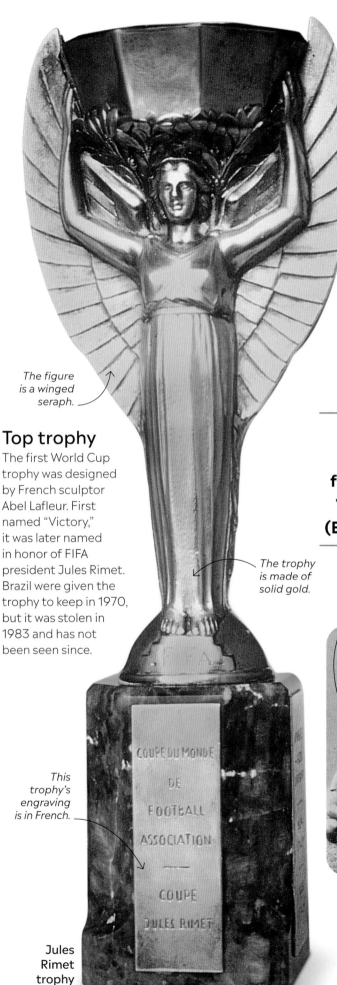

The figure is a winged seraph.

Top trophy
The first World Cup trophy was designed by French sculptor Abel Lafleur. First named "Victory," it was later named in honor of FIFA president Jules Rimet. Brazil were given the trophy to keep in 1970, but it was stolen in 1983 and has not been seen since.

The trophy is made of solid gold.

This trophy's engraving is in French.

COUPE DU MONDE
DE
FOOTBALL
ASSOCIATION
——
COUPE
JULES RIMET

Jules Rimet trophy

In 1994, American fans flocked to the matches.

Read all about it
Programs for the World Cup differ from the club variety because they cover the tournament rather than one match. They contain team information and are printed in several languages. These programs are from Sweden '58, England '66, Spain '82, Italy '90, and US '94.

The **record attendance** for a World Cup final is **173,850 fans** (Brazil v. Uruguay, 1950).

Garrincha   Didi   *Center-forward Vava*   *Pelé was 17 in 1958.*   *Left-winger Zagalo scored the fourth goal in the final.*

The beautiful game
The 1958 final saw Brazil become one of the World Cup's greatest teams. Their forward line-up was among the strongest ever. Mario Zagalo later became Brazil's manager and was in charge when they won in 1970 and 1994.

Continued on next page

Continued from previous page

We must have the World Cup

This was the poster for the 1962 finals in Chile. Earthquakes marred the run-up, but the hosts were determined. President of the Chilean FA Carlos Dittborn said, "We have nothing. That is why we must have the World Cup." Chile overcame the doubts of some European teams by staging a successful event.

A globe forms the top of the trophy.

World Cup Willie inspired a song by Lonnie Donegan.

World Cup Willie was a lion like the three lions on England's uniform.

The real trophy is 14.4 in (36.5 cm) high and weighs 13.6 lb (6.175 kg).

Designed by Italian Silvio Gazzaniga, the trophy is made of solid 18-carat gold.

New-look Cup

The present World Cup trophy was made for the 1974 finals in West Germany. After winning for the third time in 1970, Brazil could keep the Jules Rimet trophy for good. The new trophy was commissioned by FIFA.

Mascots for money

World Cup Willie was the first World Cup mascot. Designed for the 1966 tournament in England, he represented increased commercialism. Mascots now appear on official merchandise.

Replica of the World Cup trophy

Thinking positive

In 1978, hosts Argentina inspired fans with their positive attitude. The star of their winning team was Mario Kempes.

Hard work for hosts

Many countries bid to hold the World Cup years in advance. They try to convince FIFA that they can stage a successful tournament by producing information about the stadiums, transport networks, accommodations, and media facilities. Qatar won the bid to host the tournament in 2022, while the 2026 event will be jointly hosted by the US, Mexico, and Canada.

Spanish Football Federation crest

A pack of cards illustrating the stadiums.

Information pack for Spain 1982

Enthusiastic America

Despite having no strong tradition of professional soccer, the United States hosted a successful World Cup in 1994. Large and enthusiastic crowds attended the games. This is a ticket for the match between Italy and Mexico.

Who plays who?

Each ball contains a slip of paper with a team written on it.

The balls are brightly colored for the benefit of TV audiences.

Plastic balls are used to make the draw for the World Cup finals. It is a fair way to decide who plays whom. The number of teams increased from 13 in 1930 to 32 in 2014, and will feature 48 teams from 2026. The present system ensures that every team plays three games in the first round. Games are then played on a knock-out basis, until only two remain.

👁 EYEWITNESS

Megan Rapinoe
Leading US soccer player Megan Rapinoe (center) has won numerous awards, including the 2019 Ballon d'Or Féminin, Best FIFA Women's Player, and both the 2019 FIFA Women's World Cup Golden Ball and its Golden Boot. The US won their fourth FIFA Women's World Cup title in 2019, largely because of Rapinoe's skill.

The 2022 World Cup

Exceptional performances from Moroccan players such as Sofyan Amrabat and Yassine Bounou (above) saw Morocco reach the semi-final stage in Qatar 2022, becoming the first African nation to do so. In the final, France and Argentina went head to head in one of the most closely contested finals in FIFA World Cup history, with Argentina winning 4-2 after a penalty shoot-out.

Top trophies

The moment when a team captain is presented with a trophy and holds it up to the fans is the crowning glory of any campaign. Cups and trophies are the marks of success, and the managers of many modern clubs must win to keep their jobs. The desire to make money has led to the creation of many new competitions, some of which do not have the same prestige as older tournaments.

Early cup

This silver-plated trophy from the 1870s is an example of an early soccer trophy. After the FA Cup was started in 1872, similar local tournaments began to be set up in England and Scotland.

Corner flags used as decoration

Coupe des Clubs Champions Européens 1984/85

Europese Beker der Landskampioenen 1984/85

FINALE
LIVERPOOL F.C.
JUVENTUS F.C.

29.5.1985 · 20.15
Stade du Heysel · Bruxelles
Heizelstadion · Brussel

Programme officiel : 40 BF
Officieel programma

Team talk

First staged in 1956, the European Cup (now called the UEFA Champions League) was originally for the champions of each European country's league. Today, up to four teams from a nation's top domestic league can qualify for this competition. The Champions League is the most prestigious continental tournament in Europe.

Olympic soccer

This badge is from the 1956 Olympic Games. The first official Olympic soccer tournament was staged in 1908.

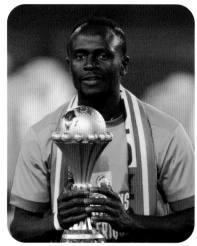

From strength to strength

The Africa Cup of Nations has been held since 1957. Although the first edition featured only three nations, 24 teams now take part. Senegal's Sadio Mane is pictured with the trophy after Senegal won 4–2 on penalties against Egypt in 2021.

Little tin idols

The first FA Cup (below left) was known as the "Little Tin Idol." It was stolen from a store display in 1895 and never recovered. The 1911 FA Cup (below right) was made in Bradford, England, and was retired in 1992.

Full house

In the 1999 Women's World Cup held in the United States, teams played to capacity crowds. The final was held in the Rose Bowl in California. Here, US player Cindy Parlow rides a tackle in the final against China, which was won by the US.

Women's World Cup

The first Women's World Cup took place in China in 1991. The tournament grew bigger and drew large crowds. This is the trophy awarded to the US in 1999.

The silver UEFA trophy is decorated with figures of soccer players.

Names of previous winners are engraved around the base.

Copa América

First held in 1916, the Copa América is one of the oldest major international tournaments. It was originally for South American nations, but Mexico and the US have also taken part. Since 2007, the tournament has been held every four years.

Second best

The UEFA (Union of European Football Associations) Cup was originally known as the Inter City Fairs Cup. It was renamed again in 2008 to what we now know as the UEFA Europa League. Teams playing in the group stages include those finishing behind domestic-league winners and winners of national cup competitions.

Playing the game

Generations of children had their first contact with soccer through toys such as board games, blow football, card games, and table soccer. The popularity of soccer drives manufacturers and inventors to come up with new products, far more than any other sport. The simplicity of toys from the past contrasts sharply with the speed, excitement, and realistic action of modern video games such as EA Sports *FIFA* and Konami *E-Football*.

Points are lost if a marble is trapped here.

Marbles are fired up this chute.

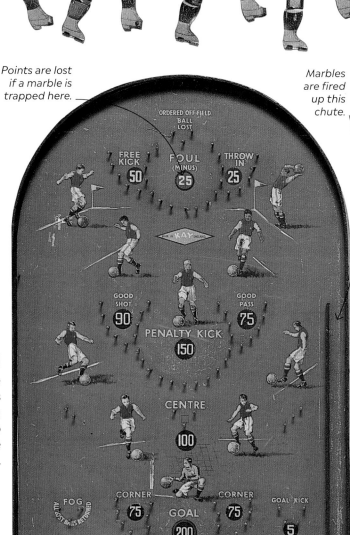

Pinball
In this tabletop game from the 1950s, players shoot marbles around the board using a spring in the corner. Points add up depending on where the marbles stop.

In the trenches
Trench Football was produced for British soldiers in World War I. The player must move a ball bearing past the German generals to score.

Ball rolling
This handheld toy from the early 20th century involves rolling the ball bearing into one of the holes.

Soccer matchbox
This is the world's smallest soccer game, probably made in Japan in the 1930s. As the matchbox opens, a spring is released and the players pop up.

EYEWITNESS

Sam Kerr
Australia and Chelsea center-forward Sam Kerr is the leading goal scorer of her country, with 110 goals. In 2022, she became the first female soccer player to feature on the cover of the global version of the EA Sports *FIFA 23 Ultimate Edition* video game.

Ball for the Kick game

Downward pressure on one leg causes the other leg to kick.

Kick figures

These figures come from a tabletop game called Kick, made in about 1900. A green cloth field and goals with nets are included. Players make the mechanical soccer players kick by pressing them down on the table.

Soccer video games

Video-game developer EA's *FIFA* series and Konami's *E-Football* are played by a wide range of fans. Many soccer clubs employ successful gamers to take part in international gaming tournaments such as the FIFA eWorld Cup, competing for a prize of $250,000.

The game's score is displayed on this cardboard scorecard.

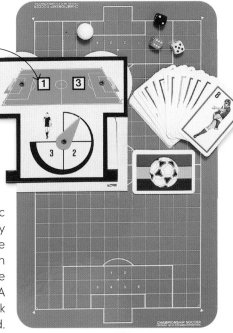

Champions!

This game, called Championship Soccer, was made in 1983. It uses two of the classic components of many board games—dice and cards—to govern the movement of the ball around the field. A scoreboard and clock are also included.

Playing indoors

Tabletop foosball and Subbuteo, the flick-to-kick game, are hugely popular around the world and are played by fans of all ages. Many people also collect Match Attax cards, the world's most popular soccer-card-trading game.

Players move and rotate these revolving rods to flick the ball into the opponent's goal and to defend their own goal.

Poster painting
In this advertising card from the 1920s, an Italian drink company has illustrated its product in a soccer scene.

VERMOUTH JACCOBINO

Baines cards
These cards from the late 19th and early 20th century were the forerunners of sticker albums. They featured soccer and rugby league teams at professional and amateur level.

Wednesday, now Sheffield Wednesday

Scottish club Hearts

Chadderton, a nonleague team

Memorabilia

Soccer can be used to promote a range of items. Soccer-related advertising and product promotion is nothing new. Companies were latching onto the game's popularity in the early 20th century. An understated style and original artwork dominated until the 1950s. This has been replaced by mass-produced items, reliant on star players and wealthy clubs.

Covered stands are rare in southern Europe.

Sports tin
By the 1930s, original artwork with a sports theme was often used as a decoration for household items. This tin features soccer on the lid and other sports on the outside.

1910 silver case advertising the mustard-maker Colman's

Souvenirs
Mementos of the World Cup finals do not stop at programs and tickets. Many souvenirs are also popular, such as these erasers featuring the logos of the 1990 World Cup in Italy.

Healthy kick
There is no magic soccer ingredient in this drink, but the manufacturers knew that any association with soccer would improve sales.

Soccer fan
This Spanish lady's fan from the mid-20th century has a soccer image on one side and a promotional message on the back. Many commercial objects were designed to be artistic as well as functional.

CORONA BRAND FOOTBALL STOUT THOMAS & EVANS LTD PORTH.

Team train

In the 1980s, the Hornby toy company of Liverpool, England, produced a series of these scale models of the London North Eastern Railway's locomotives, named after soccer clubs. This is the *Manchester United*. Real trains can be named after clubs.

Name plate

Banks Johnstone Jennings England Best

Petrol heads

The Cleveland Petrol company produced these miniatures of British international players in 1971.

Olympic clock

This German wooden clock may have been made to commemorate the 1936 Berlin Olympics. This soccer tournament was won by Italy, when they beat Austria 2–1 in the final. The figures at the top move on the hour.

Pocket watch

Watch

Full-time

This group includes a Swiss pocket watch made in Geneva around 1910, a British watch from the 1950s, and a more modern 1970s alarm clock. Design and materials, and therefore cost, were dictated by whether the object was aimed at children or adults.

Alarm clock

Chain

Locket

String along

Made in the 1880s, this copper string-holder stops string from getting tangled.

The mold is made up of two parts.

Compass

Chain medals

Soccer items are often turned into jewelry. Four silver medals from the 1920s are attached to this chain. The silver locket and compass are both from the 1880s.

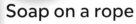

Soap on a rope

The Avon company produced this soap soccer ball to mark the 1966 World Cup.

Chocolate

Melted chocolate would have been poured into this early 20th-century brass mold and left to cool and set, producing a miniature chocolate soccer player with a ball at his feet. This item was made to appeal mainly to children.

The business of **soccer**

Soccer is big business. Millions of fans attend matches, club products sell worldwide, and top players and managers earn big wages. The clubs of the 1880s provided cheap entertainment for the public and offered a decent living to players. Today, club owners and star players stretch the money-making potential to the limit.

Billy's bribe

This shirt was worn by Welshman Billy Meredith. As a player for Manchester City, England, he was banned for a year in 1905 for allegedly trying to bribe a rival captain with $48 (£10) to lose a big game. This was soccer's first major scandal.

Ground force

Advertising in and around soccer grounds was allowed long before shirt sponsorship. In the 1950s, it featured mainly local firms, but now larger multinational companies exploit the exposure provided by television coverage. Billboards at top-level clubs are now electronic, rotating to catch the eye of the public and to allow more advertisers to use the limited space.

In 2017, Salah moved from AS Roma to Liverpool FC for a fee of around $43.5 million.

All abroad!

Political and legal changes have made it easy for soccer players to move abroad and play for foreign clubs. Players from overseas, such as Egyptian forward Mohamed Salah, are often the star players of England's Premier League clubs.

Under stress

Modern managers experience stress and have to accept that every decision will be examined by the media. In most major leagues, a manager is expected to produce a winning team within months. In 2020, former England international player Wayne Rooney became interim player-manager of Derby County and won his debut game as manager 2–1. He served as full-time manager from 2021 to 2022.

Keep your shirt on

Replica shirts are a big source of income for famous clubs such as England's Manchester United (below) and Spain's Real Madrid. At least three designs are available at one time. Clubs produce hundreds of products—from calendars to baby clothes. These can be sold to fans all over the world, reducing the club's reliance on gate receipts.

Europe v. South America

The Intercontinental Cup was contested by the top team in Europe and the top team in South America. Originally a home-and-away fixture won by the team with the highest aggregate score, it was changed to a single fixture in 1980. The cup was called the FIFA Club World Championships in 2005 before being rebranded as the FIFA Club World Cup in 2006.

FIFA Club World Cup

Kylian Mbappé
French forward Kylian Mbappé joined Paris Saint-Germain for a record $206-million deal in 2017. His 2022 contract with the club made him the world's highest-paid soccer player, reportedly being paid over $1 million a week.

Media moguls

Media tycoon and former Italian prime minister Silvio Berlusconi bought AC Milan in 1986, when soccer's television coverage was increasing. He maximized commercial opportunities and attracted stars from abroad before selling the club in 2016.

Shirt ads

Companies have paid soccer clubs to put their logos on shirts since the 1970s. Barcelona only began a commercial relationship for the first time in 2010, resulting in a sponsorship from Qatar Airways that lasted until 2017. In 2022, they signed a sponsorship deal with music-streaming service Spotify.

The science of soccer

For many years, soccer was not a subject of scientific investigation, so coaches and players relied on knowledge from experience. Over time, nutritionists transformed players' diets, physicists studied how to bend the ball, and information technology has made a statistical analysis of the game. Advancing technology has made its mark on soccer, while our growing understanding of sports science and sports psychology has impacted team performance.

Training muscles

Training was once a few laps around the field, but advances in medical science have produced highly specialized regimes. Players warm up and cool down to avoid muscle strain and do specific work on muscle groups to cope with the range of moves.

Isotonic nutrition

Soccer players can lose up to 7 pints (3 liters) of water during a game, so it is imperative that they rehydrate their bodies during and after a match. Isotonic drinks, which contain small amounts of salts and sugars, are the most effective at doing this. They also help replenish a player's spent calories.

Strength and fitness

Elite soccer players follow a strict training program. Each player may have an individual development plan, with fitness targets to help them improve their performance and increase their stamina.

Barcelona player Asisat Oshoala

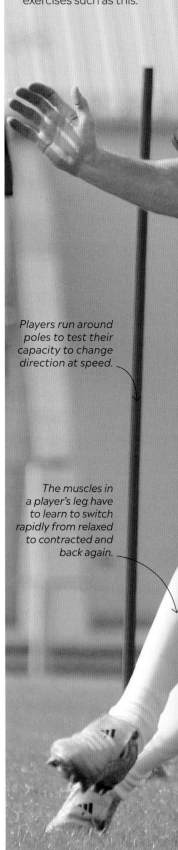

Physical demands

The German national team were put through their paces before the 2006 World Cup. Their levels of fitness were monitored and recorded in training exercises such as this.

Players run around poles to test their capacity to change direction at speed.

The muscles in a player's leg have to learn to switch rapidly from relaxed to contracted and back again.

Eyes in the sky

Did all of the ball cross all of the line? New technology such as fast-frame cameras and magnetic circuits can now track a ball's movement in the goal area and relay the information to a computer, which determines whether the ball has crossed the goal-line.

Wearable technology

Vests (left) and other accessories can be made into GPS-enabled wearable technology to monitor a player's performance and gain a competitive edge over their rivals. The performance data is used to see where players can make improvements to aspects of their fitness, such as speed, strength, and power.

Beeping flags

Assistant referees use flags to attract the referee's attention. If something is missed, the assistant can press a button on the flag's handle. The referee's receiver, which is strapped to the arm, will then vibrate or beep.

Did you **know?**

AMAZING FACTS

On average, each player in a match has the ball for only three minutes, the time it takes to boil an egg!

In 1965, substitutes were allowed for the first time, but only when a player was injured. Substitutes featured in the World Cup for the first time in 1970. Luis Chilavert, goalkeeper for Paraguay, rushed out of his goal and scored for his team against Argentina in 1998. The final score was 1–1.

In 1974, Holland's Johan Neeskens was the first player to score a penalty in a World Cup final.

Johann Cruyff's mother was a cleaner for the club Ajax in Holland. When she asked them to give her 10-year-old son a trial, they signed him as a youth player. He became an international star.

The goal net came to be in use from 1895. The crossbar was introduced in 1875.

The first time teams used numbered shirts in an FA Cup final was in 1933. Everton wore numbers 1 to 11, and Manchester City wore numbers 12 to 22.

Eight of the players who won the World Cup for Brazil in 1958 were in the team that retained the World Cup in 1962.

Only eight different countries have been World Cup champions, although there have been 22 tournaments.

The FA Cup is soccer's oldest competition. The highest-scoring FA Cup victory was in 1887, when Preston North End beat Hyde United 26–0 in the first round of the competition.

Two pairs of brothers, John and Mel Charles and Len and Ivor Allchurch, played in the Welsh team that beat Northern Ireland 3–2 in 1955.

Uruguay, with a population of just 3 million, is the smallest nation to have won the World Cup (in 1930 and 1950).

Uruguayan forward Héctor Castro, who had an amputated right arm, scored his nation's first-ever World Cup goal in 1930, as well as the winner that won them the tournament.

The first international soccer match played by a side with 12 players was in 1952, between France and Northern Ireland. One of the French players was injured and substituted, but after treatment, he kept playing and no one noticed until halftime.

Son Heung-min playing for English club Tottenham Hotspur

Half of the world's registered soccer players are from Asia. South Korean forward Son Heung-min is one of the leading stars playing in Europe.

Pelé scored 1,283 goals during his senior career.

Only seven clubs have managed to win the English Premier League since its current version was created in 1992.

Manchester City lift the Premier League trophy in 2022.

QUESTIONS AND ANSWERS

Which is the most successful international women's team?

The United States, which won the World Cup in 1991, 1999, 2015, and 2019. Germany has won two World Cups (2003, 2007) and hosted it in 2011. The US were runners-up once, in 2011, and have claimed Olympic gold four times—in 1996, 2004, 2008, and 2012.

Why was the first World Cup held in Uruguay?

The other applicants (Hungary, Italy, Spain, the Netherlands, and Sweden) withdrew their bids.

When were floodlights first used?

The first recorded use of floodlights was at Bramall Lane, Sheffield, England, in 1878. The lamps were placed on wooden gantries and were powered by dynamos.

When were women banned from playing at FA clubs?

In 1920, around 46,000 fans packed into Goodison Park to watch Dick Kerr Ladies play St. Helens Ladies. The FA, worried that the women's game was socially unacceptable, banned women from playing on FA club grounds in 1921. The ban was not lifted until 1970!

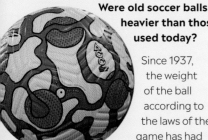

Were old soccer balls heavier than those used today?

Since 1937, the weight of the ball according to the laws of the game has had to be 14–16 oz (397–454 g).

Modern soccer ball

Which country was the first to be knocked out of a World Cup in a penalty shoot-out?

Penalty shoot-outs were introduced at the World Cup finals in 1982, when West Germany knocked out France.

Who plays soccer in the Olympics?

The national women's soccer teams compete in the Olympic Games, but for men, only the national under-23 teams take part.

Alexandra Popp of Germany

Who was England's first Black professional soccer player?

Arthur Wharton, originally from Ghana, played for Preston North End as an amateur in the 1880s and as a professional for Rotherham Town, Sheffield United, and Stockport County.

Why have there been five FA Cup trophies?

The first trophy was stolen from a sports store in Birmingham, England. When Manchester United won the FA Cup in 1909, they copied the trophy for a director. The FA withdrew this trophy and made a third FA Cup. Due to damage, this was replaced with a replica in 1992. The 1992 version of the cup was replaced in 2014 with the current (fifth) trophy.

What does the phrase "back to square one" have to do with soccer?

When the BBC first broadcast soccer live on radio in 1927, the *Radio Times* magazine printed a diagram of the field, divided into numbered squares. When the ball was passed back to the goalkeeper, the commentators said, "Back to square one."

BBC radio microphone

RECORD-BREAKERS

⚽ Brazil is the only country to have played in the final stages of every World Cup.

⚽ The oldest soccer club in the world that still exists today is Sheffield FC. Formed in 1857, the club has always played nonleague soccer.

⚽ Lev Yashin (Russia) is the only goalkeeper to win European Footballer of the Year.

⚽ In 1999, Manchester United made history by becoming the first team to win the Treble of the Premier League, the FA Cup, and the European Champions League.

⚽ Real Madrid have won the European Champions League 14 times, more than any other team.

⚽ At the age of 15 years and 181 days, Ethan Nwaneri of Arsenal became the youngest-ever player to play in the Premier League when he came on as a substitute in a 2022 Premier League match.

Ethan Nwaneri playing for Arsenal

Who's who?

Soccer is a game of speed and skill, with many outstanding players. In international competitions such as the FIFA World Cup, extensive media coverage means soccer players from around the world can become household names. Referees can also build up a global reputation. These pages contain some of the past, present, and upcoming players who are among the world's best.

Italian referee Pierluigi Collina

GOALKEEPERS

Peter Schmeichel, Denmark, b.11-18-1963 Schmeichel moved to Manchester United in 1991, where he won five league titles and two FA Cups. In his trademark "star" save, Schmeichel runs out, spreads his arms and legs wide, and jumps toward the striker.

Gianluigi Buffon, Italy, b.1-28-1978 A World Cup winner with Italy in 2006, Buffon became the world's most expensive goalkeeper in 2001, when Juventus paid Parma $45 million (£32.6 million).

Iker Casillas, Spain, b.5-20-1981 Casillas made his debut for Spanish club Real Madrid in 1999 at age 17 and stayed there until 2015. He was captain of Spain for their 2010 World Cup and European Championship successes in 2008 and 2012.

Iker Casillas

Jan Oblak, Slovenia, b.1-7-1993 One of the best goalkeepers in the world, Oblak's shot-stopping is immense. With Atletico Madrid, he holds the record for the fewest goals conceded in a season (18 goals in 35 games).

Ederson Moraes, Brazil, b.8-17-1993 Ederson began his senior career at Benfica in 2015. Recognized for his excellent ball distribution and ability to make reflex saves, he secured a move to Manchester City in 2017.

DEFENDERS

Paolo Maldini

Paolo Maldini, Italy, b.6-26-1968 Attacking fullback Maldini captained AC Milan and Italy, appearing for Italy over 120 times.

Marcel Desailly, France, b.9-7-1968 Born in Accra, Ghana, Desailly moved to France as a child. In 1993 and 1994, he won the Champions League, with Marseille and then AC Milan. Desailly played a vital role in the French national team when they won the 1998 World Cup and the European Championship in 2000.

Roberto Carlos da Silva, Brazil, b.4-10-1973 With a reputation for ferocious free kicks, Roberto Carlos entered the Brazilian national team after the 1994 World Cup. A runner-up in 1998, he won the World Cup in 2002. He joined Real Madrid in 1996, winning the Spanish league in his first season.

Fabio Cannavaro, Italy, b.9-13-1973 Although small, Cannavaro was a tenacious defender. He captained Italy to World Cup glory in 2006, and the same year became the first defender to win the FIFA World Player of the Year award.

Sergio Ramos, Spain, b.3-30-1986 A World Cup winner in 2010 and a two-time winner of the European Championships, Paris Saint Germain's Ramos has been present for Spain since his debut in 2005.

Virgil Van Dijk, Netherlands, b.7-8-1991 One of the game's greatest defenders, Van Dijk has mastered the center-half role. He has demonstrated excellent strength, composure, and aerial ability, both for Liverpool and the Netherlands.

Kalidou Koulibaly, Senegal, b.6-28-1991 Koulibaly is a club legend at Napoli, winning several awards and drawing attention for his work to combat social injustice, inequality, and racism. He moved to Chelsea in 2022.

Leah Williamson, England, b.3-29-1997 Captain of England's women's team, Leah Williamson is a versatile defender who can also play in midfield. Her outstanding range of passing and ability to evade pressure contributed to England's Women's Euro 2022 win.

Leah Williamson

MIDFIELDERS

Luis Filipe Madeira Caeiro Figo, Portugal, b.11-4-1972
Figo was a European champion at under-16 level in 1989 and a World Youth Cup winner in 1991. He won the Portuguese Cup with Sporting Clube in 1995 and moved to Barcelona, where he captained them to the Spanish league title in 1998 before playing for Real Madrid.

Andrea Pirlo, Italy, b.5-19-1979
One of the game's great passers, Pirlo enjoyed success at national and international level. He won the Champions League with AC Milan twice and the World Cup with Italy in 2006.

Andrea Pirlo

Andrés Iniesta, Spain, b.5-11-1984
A product of the famous Barcelona youth academy, Andrés Iniesta's ability to pass, shoot, and score singles him

out as a complete attacking midfielder. He has won four Champions League titles with Barcelona, two European Championships, and one World Cup.

Luka Modric, Croatia, b.9-9-1985
Captain of the Croatia team, Luka Modric is considered to be the country's greatest soccer player ever. The Real Madrid midfielder won the Ballon d'Or in 2018.

Kevin De Bruyne, Belgium, b.6-28-1991
Described by experts as a complete soccer player, De Bruyne has more than 90 caps for Belgium, four Premier League titles, five League cups, and an FA Cup win with Manchester City.

N'golo Kante, France, b.3-29-1991
Known for his defensive understanding and high work rate, Kante is the first outfield player to win consecutive league titles, winning with Leicester City in 2016 and Chelsea in 2017.

Lieke Martens, Netherlands, b.12-16-1992
Dutch midfielder Martens is one of the most complete, technical players in women's soccer. She plays for French club Paris Saint Germain.

Pablo Martín Páez Gavira, Spain, b.8-5-2004
Popularly known as Gavi, the Spanish midfielder is a technically gifted player with a winning mentality. He joined Barcelona's Academy at age 11 and made his senior club and International debut for Spain at just 17 years of age in 2021.

Gavi

FORWARDS

Roberto Baggio, Italy, b.2-18-1967
A gifted goal scorer, Baggio helped Juventus win the UEFA Cup in 1993 and the league title in 1995. He was FIFA's World Player of the Year and European Footballer of the Year for 1993.

Marco van Basten, Netherlands, b.10-31-1964
Goal-machine van Basten was a three-time Ballon d'Or winner, won the European Cup twice with Milan, and took the Netherlands to victory at the 1988 European Championships. An ankle injury at age 28 made him retire.

Ronaldo Luis Nazario, Brazil, b.9-22-1976
Ronaldo scored his first goal for Brazil when he was only 16. An inspirational striker, his speed and skill could break

Marta

through almost any defense. He was World Player of the Year in 1996, 1997, and 2002.

Thierry Henry, France, b.8-17-1977
A striker with terrific ball control, incredible pace, and clinical finishing, Henry was top goal scorer for France when they won the World Cup in 1998.

Sunil Chettri, India, b.8-3-1984
Captain of India and Bengaluru FC, Chettri is the country's all-time top goal scorer (84 goals in 131 appearances). He is the most decorated soccer player in India.

Marta, Brazil, b.12-9-1986
Marta is considered the greatest female player of all time, having won the FIFA Women's World Player of the Year award six times.

Harry Kane, England, b.7-28-1993
England and Tottenham striker Harry Kane is a prolific goal scorer for both club and country, scoring 319 career goals.

Asisat Oshoala, Nigeria, b.9-9-1994
Nigeria and Barcelona striker Oshoala is a very effective physical presence on the field, using her extensive strength, dribbling, and finishing ability to be ruthless and deadly in the box.

Erling Haaland, Norway, b.7-21-2000
An exciting forward with excellent agility, balance, and strength, Haaland's goal-scoring record at Borussia Dortmund propelled him to superstar status, resulting in a move to Manchester City in 2022.

Erling Haaland

World Cup wins

The FIFA Men's World Cup began in 1930. In 2018, a global audience of 1.1 billion people tuned in to watch the final. The Cup's history is packed with super scorers, memorable moments, and amazing anecdotes.

HIGH SCORES

⚽ The highest score in the World Cup finals was when Hungary beat El Salvador 10-1 in 1982.

⚽ The highest score in a World Cup qualifier came in 2001, when Australia beat American Samoa 31-0.

GREATEST GOAL SCORERS

Miroslav Klose (Germany)
16 goals 2002–2014

Ronaldo (Brazil)
15 goals 1994–2006

Gerd Muller (West Germany)
14 goals 1966–1974

Lionel Messi (Argentina)
13 goals 2005–present

Just Fontaine (France)
13 goals 1958

Pelé (Brazil)
12 goals 1958–1970

Jürgen Klinsmann (Germany)
11 goals 1990–1998

Thomas Müller (Germany)
10 goals 2010–2022

Brazil's Ronaldo

WINNERS

Only eight countries have ever lifted the World Cup trophy:

Brazil	1958, 1962, 1970, 1994, 2002
Italy	1934, 1938, 1982, 2006
Germany	1954, 1974, 1990, 2014
Argentina	1978, 1986, 2022
Uruguay	1930, 1950
France	1998, 2018
England	1966
Spain	2010

Royal request
At the first World Cup held in Uruguay in 1930, the Romanian squad was handpicked by King Carol, who organized time off work for the players!

Barefeet
India qualified for the 1950 World Cup in Brazil but had to withdraw, as FIFA would not let them compete barefoot.

It's a knockout
At the 1958 World Cup finals, the Brazilian player Vava scored against the Soviet Union. His teammates mobbed him with such enthusiasm that he was left unconscious!

Oldest player
Egypt's Essam El-Hadary was 45 at the 2018 World Cup.

Youngest player
Brazil's Edú was 16 years and 11 months old at the 1966 World Cup.

FASTEST GOALS AFTER KICKOFF

Hakan Sukur	(TURKEY) v. SOUTH KOREA 2002	11 seconds
Vaclav Masek	(CZECHOSLOVAKIA) v. MEXICO 1962	15 seconds
Ernst Lehner	(GERMANY) v. AUSTRIA 1934	25 seconds
Bryan Robson	(ENGLAND) v. FRANCE 1982	28 seconds
Clint Dempsey	(USA) v. GHANA 2014	29 seconds

TROPHY TRIVIA

NEW TROPHY

The existing World Cup trophy was first awarded in 1974. The name and year of every World Cup winner is added to the bottom of the trophy. In 2038, a new trophy will be needed because there will not be enough space left for new names.

The trophy is made of 18-carat gold! It is 14.4 in (36.5 cm) high and weighs 13.6 lb (6.175 kg).

OLD TROPHY

The original trophy was called the Jules Rimet Trophy in honor of the FIFA president from 1921 to 1954. The Frenchman set up the first World Cup finals in 1930.

The Jules Rimet Trophy was stolen twice. The first theft was in England in 1966, but a dog named Pickles later discovered it. The trophy was then stolen again in Rio de Janeiro in 1983 but never found.

STADIUMS

The first World Cup final, in Uruguay in 1930, was held in the Estadio Centenario in Montevideo. It had a capacity of just under 100,000 spectators, with many standing.

The final of the 2014 World Cup took place in the Estádio do Maracanã in Rio de Janeiro. One of the most recognizable stadiums in world soccer, the Maracanã was built for the 1950 World Cup. It is believed to have once held around 200,000 spectators, but its current capacity is 78,000.

The 2018 World Cup was held at 12 stadiums located all across Russia, from St. Petersburg in the north of the country to Sochi, 1,460 miles (2,350 km) to the south.

The 2022 World Cup in Qatar was held across eight stadiums, each capable of seating more than 40,000 spectators. The final was played in front of 80,000 people at the Lusail Stadium (below) near Doha.

Italy lift the World Cup in 2006

Penalty shoot-out
Italy won the World Cup final in 2006, beating France 5-3 on penalties. To date, only three finals have been decided by penalties—1994, 2006, and 2022.

Global audience

The World Cup draws one of the largest audiences of any televised event on Earth and is viewed in stadiums and public squares, in homes, and even on smartphones. The 2018 World Cup in Russia was broadcast in every country in the world and the final of the tournament is estimated to have been viewed by an audience of 1.1 billion.

National teams

The "beautiful game" is played all over the world on streets, on fields, at beaches, and in parks. In each country, the most gifted players join their national teams to compete in high-profile tournaments.

 ## ENGLAND

FOOTBALL ASSOCIATION FOUNDED: 1863
NICKNAMES: Men's team—The Three Lions; Women's team—The Lionesses
TOP GOAL SCORER: Men's team—Wayne Rooney 53 (2003-2016); Women's team—Ellen White 52 (2010-2022)
MOST APPEARANCES: Men's team—Peter Shilton 125 (1970-1990); Women's team—Fara Williams 172 (2001-2019)
TROPHIES: FIFA World Cup—1966; UEFA Women's Euro—2022

 ## ARGENTINA

ARGENTINIAN FOOTBALL ASSOCIATION FOUNDED: 1893
NICKNAMES: Men's and Women's teams—*Albicelestes* (White and Sky Blues)
TOP GOAL SCORER: Lionel Messi 98 (2005-present)
MOST APPEARANCES: Lionel Messi 172 (2005-present)
TROPHIES: FIFA World Cup—1978, 1986, 2022; Copa América—1921, 1925, 1927, 1929, 1937, 1941, 1945, 1946, 1947, 1955, 1957, 1959 (round-robin league tournaments), 1991 (round-robin), 1993, 2021; CONMEBOL—1993, 2021; Olympic Gold Medal—2004, 2008

 ## FRANCE

FRENCH FEDERATION OF FOOTBALL FOUNDED: 1919
NICKNAMES: Men's team—*Les Bleus* (The Blues); Women's team—*Les Bleuses* (The Blues)
TOP GOAL SCORER: Men's team—Olivier Giroud 53 (2011-present); Women's team—Eugenie Le Sommer 86 (2009-present)
MOST APPEARANCES: Men's team—Lilian Thuram 142 (1994-2008); Women's team—Sandrine Soubeyrand 198 (1997-2013)
TROPHIES: FIFA World Cup—1998, 2018; UEFA Euro—1984, 2000; Olympic Gold Medal—1984; FIFA Confederations Cup—2001, 2003

 ## AUSTRALIA

AUSTRALIAN SOCCER ASSOCIATION FOUNDED: 1961
NICKNAMES: Men's team—Socceroos; Women's team—The Matildas
TOP GOAL SCORER: Men's team—Tim Cahill 50 (2004-present); Women's team—Sam Kerr 59 (2000-present)
MOST APPEARANCES: Men's team—Mark Schwarzer 109 (1993-2013); Women's team—Cheryl Salisbury 151 (1994-2009)
TROPHIES: OFC Nations Cup—1980, 1996, 2000, 2004; AFC Asian Cup—2015; OFC Women's Championships—1994, 1998, 2003; AFF Women's Championships—2008; AFC Women's Asia Cup—2010

 ## GERMANY

GERMAN FOOTBALL ASSOCIATION FOUNDED: 1900
NICKNAMES: Men's team—*Die Mannschaft* (The Team); Women's team—DFB *Frauenteam* (DFB Women's Team)
TOP GOAL SCORER: Men's team—Miroslav Klose 71 (2001-2014); Women's team—Birgit Prinz 128 (1994-2011)
MOST APPEARANCES: Men's team—Lothar Matthaus 150 (1980-2000); Women's team—Birgit Prinz 214 (1994-2011)
TROPHIES: FIFA World Cup—1954, 1974, 1990, 2014; UEFA Euro—1972, 1980, 1996; Olympic Gold Medal—1976; FIFA Women's World Cup 2003, 2007; UEFA Women's Euro—1989, 1991, 1995, 1997, 2011, 2005, 2009, 2013

 ## BRAZIL

BRAZILIAN SOCCER ASSOCIATION FOUNDED: 1914
NICKNAMES: Men's team—*A Seleção* (The Selected), *Canarinho* (Little Canary); Women's team—*Seleção* (The Selected), *As Canarinhas* (The Female Canaries)
TOP GOAL SCORER: Men's team—Pelé 77 (1957-1971), Neymar 77 (2010-present); Women's team—Marta 115 (2003-present)
MOST APPEARANCES: Men's team—Cafu 142 (1990-2006); Women's team—Formiga 206 (1995-2021)
TROPHIES: FIFA World Cup—1958, 1962, 1970, 1994, 2002; Copa América—1919, 1922, 1949, 1989, 1997, 1999, 2004, 2007, 2019; Copa América Femenina—1991, 1995, 1998, 2006, 2010, 2014, 2018

 ## ITALY

ITALIAN FOOTBALL FEDERATION FOUNDED: 1898
NICKNAMES: Men's team—*Azzurri* (Blues); Women's team—*Le Azzure* (Blues)
TOP GOAL SCORER: Men's team—Luigi Riva 35 (1965-1974); Women's team—Elisabetta Vignotto 107 (1970-1989), Patrizia Panaco 107 (1996-2014)
MOST APPEARANCES: Men's team—Gianluigi Buffon 176 (1997-2018); Women's team—Patrizia Panaco 196 (1996-2014)
TROPHIES: FIFA World Cup—1934, 1938, 1982, 2006; UEFA Euro—1968, 2020; Olympic Gold Medal—1936

IVORY COAST

IVORY COAST FOOTBALL FEDERATION FOUNDED: 1960
NICKNAMES: *Les Elephants* (The Elephants)
TOP GOAL SCORER: Didier Drogba 65 (2002–2014)
MOST APPEARANCES: Didier Zokora 123 (2000–2014)
TROPHIES: Africa Cup of Nations—1992, 2015

JAPAN

JAPAN FOOTBALL FEDERATION FOUNDED: 1921
NICKNAMES: Men's team—Samurai Blue; Women's team—*Nadeshiko* Japan (Japan Women)
TOP GOAL SCORER: Men's team—Kunishige Kamamoto 80 (1964–1977); Women's team—Homare Sawa 83 (1993–2015)
MOST APPEARANCES: Men's team—Yasuhito Endo 152 (2002–2015); Women's team—Homare Sawa 205 (1993–2015)
TROPHIES: AFC Asian Cup—1992, 2000, 2004, 2011; AFC Women's Asian Cup—2014, 2018

KOREA REPUBLIC

KOREA FOOTBALL ASSOCIATION FOUNDED: 1928
NICKNAMES: Men's team—*Taegeuk* Warriors; Women's team—*Taegeuk* Ladies
TOP GOAL SCORER: Men's team—Cha Bum-Kun 58 (1972–1986); Women's team—Ji So-yun 61 (2006–present)
MOST APPEARANCES: Men's team—Hong Myung-Bo 136 (1990–2002), Cha Bum-Kun 136 (1972–1986); Women's team—Cho Sohyun 126 (2007–present)
TROPHIES: AFC Asian Cup—1956, 1960

MEXICO

MEXICAN FOOTBALL FEDERATION FOUNDED: 1927
NICKNAMES: Men's team—*El Tri* (The Tricolor); Women's team—*La Tri* (The Tricolor)
TOP GOAL SCORER: Men's team—Javier Hernandez 52 (2009–present); Women's team—Maribel Dominguez 82 (1998–2016)
MOST APPEARANCES: Men's team—Claudio Suarez 177 (1992–2006); Women's team—Maribel Dominguez 116 (1998–2016)
TROPHIES: CONCACAF Championship and Gold Cup—1965, 1971, 1977, 1993, 1996, 1998, 2003, 2009, 2011, 2015, 2019; FIFA Confederation Cup—1999; Olympic Gold Medal—2012

NETHERLANDS

ROYAL NETHERLANDS FOOTBALL ASSOCIATION FOUNDED: 1889
NICKNAMES: Men's and Women's teams—*Oranje* (The Oranges)
TOP GOAL SCORER: Men's team—Robin van Persie 50 (2005–2017); Women's team—Vivianne Miedema 94 (2013–present)
MOST APPEARANCES: Men's team—Wesley Sneijder 134 (2003–2018); Women's team—Sherida Spitse 206 (2006–present)
TROPHIES: UEFA Euro—1988

SOUTH AFRICA

SOUTH AFRICAN FOOTBALL ASSOCIATION FOUNDED: 1991
NICKNAMES: Men's team—Bafana Bafana (The Boys); Women's team—Banyana Banyana (The Girls)
TOP GOAL SCORER: Men's team—Benni McCarthy 31 (1997–2012); Women's team—Portia Modise 101 (2000–2015)
MOST APPEARANCES: Men's team—Aaron Mokoena 107 (1999–2010); Women's team—Janine van Wyk 170 (2005–present)
TROPHIES: Africa Cup of Nations—1996

SPAIN

ROYAL SPANISH FOOTBALL FEDERATION FOUNDED: 1913
NICKNAMES: Men's team—*La Furia Roja* (The Red Fury); Women's team—*La Roja* (The Red One)
TOP GOAL SCORER: Men's team—David Villa 59 (2005–2017); Women's team—Jennifer Hermoso 45 (2011–present)
MOST APPEARANCES: Men's team—Sergio Ramos 180 (2005–present); Women's team—Alexia Putellas 100 (2013–present)
TROPHIES: FIFA World Cup—2010; UEFA Euro—1964, 2008, 2012; Olympic Gold Medal—1992

URUGUAY

URUGUAY FOOTBALL FEDERATION FOUNDED: 1900
NICKNAMES: Men's team—*La Celeste* (The Sky Blues); Women's team—*Las Celestas* (The Sky Blues)
TOP GOAL SCORER: Men's team—Luis Suárez 68 (2007–present); Women's team—Angélica Souza 4 (2003–2006)
MOST APPEARANCES: Men's team—Diego Godín 159 (2005–present); Women's team—Aída Camaño 12 (2003–present)
TROPHIES: FIFA World Cup—1930, 1950; Copa América—1916, 1917, 1920, 1923, 1924, 1926, 1935, 1942, 1956, 1959, 1967, 1983, 1987, 1995, 2011; Olympic Gold Medal—1924, 1928

USA

UNITED STATES SOCCER FEDERATION FOUNDED: 1913
NICKNAMES: Men's team—Stars and stripes, USMNT; Women's team—Stars and stripes, USWNT
TOP GOAL SCORER: Men's team—Landon Donovan 57 (2000–2014), Clint Dempsey 57 (2004–2017); Women's team—Abby Wambach 184 (2001–2015)
MOST APPEARANCES: Men's team—Cobi Jones 164 (1992–2004); Women's team—Kristine Lilly 354 (1987–2010)
TROPHIES: FIFA Women's World Cup—1991, 1999, 2015, 2019; CONCACAF Women's Gold Cup—1991, 1993, 1994, 2000, 2002, 2006, 2014, 2018, 2022; Olympic Gold Medal (Women's team)—1996, 2004, 2008, 2012; CONCACAF Men's Gold Cup—1991, 2002, 2005, 2007, 2013, 2017, 2021; CONCACAF Nations League—2019–2020

Find out **more**

There are many ways of getting more involved in soccer. Find a club you want to support and follow their match results. If you are eager to play yourself, join a team and take part in a local league. You will find out about managers, coaches, and famous players by watching games, by visiting museums, and on the internet. The more you learn, the more you might enjoy the soccer fever surrounding big competitions.

USEFUL WEBSITES

- **To find out about the Football Association:**
  www.thefa.com
- **For information on the World Cup:**
  www.fifa.com
- **For up-to-date soccer information:**
  news.bbc.co.uk/sport/football
- **For playing tips and video classes:**
  news.bbc.co.uk/sport1/hi/football/skills
- **For informative videos on soccer:**
  theathletic.com/author/tifo-football
- **For information on women's soccer:**
  www.herfootballhub.com

Match program
Programs are full of information about the teams that are playing and are a great keepsake.

Bob Bishop was the Manchester United scout who discovered George Best, Sammy McIlroy, and many others in the 1960s and 1970s.

Soccer scouts
All big clubs have scouts who travel around looking for new talent, from established soccer players to buy, to gifted youth players. Outstanding young players are asked for a trial and may be invited to join the club's soccer academy, where they receive an education and soccer training. If all goes well, they work through the youth and reserve sides to the first team.

Support your club
Choose the club you want to support and start following their results. If you can, go to some matches and start your own collection of programs. Watching the matches and reading the programs will soon make you an expert on your club's players and management. You will learn about soccer rules and develop your own ideas on team tactics.

Italian fans cheering on their team

Join a team

If you are eager to play the game, then join a school or local youth-club team, and you will quickly find out whether you prefer defense, midfield, attack, or playing in goal. Club coaches will help you master many techniques, such as marking, tackling, dribbling, and passing. Regular training and practice games will ensure you are fit and have the stamina to last the match.

Jhoneiker Abreu of Peru controlling the ball

Soccer for all

Soccer is a game for anyone to play, anywhere and at any time. Organizations around the world create opportunities for everyone to have a fantastic experience playing soccer at grassroots, local, or international level, regardless of disability, age, gender, ethnicity, sexuality, ability, or faith.

PLACES TO VISIT

FIFA Museum, Zurich, Switzerland
www.fifamuseum.com
This collection of historic documents, videos, and pictures tells the story of how soccer became the most popular sport.

German Football Museum, Dortmund, Germany
www.fussballmuseum.de
The national museum for German soccer

Wembley Stadium, London, England
www.bookings.wembleytours.com/stadiumtours/home.htm
A collection that includes memorabilia from England's 1966 World Cup victory

Football Faentasium, Seoul World Cup Stadium, Seoul, South Korea
www.faentasium.com
Founded by the Korean Football Association, this interactive museum showcases soccer culture and celebrates the World Cup's history.

Museu do Futebol, São Paulo, Brazil
www.museudofutebol.org.br
Housed inside the Pacaembu Stadium, the museum tells the story of soccer in Brazil.

National Soccer Hall of Fame, Texas, US
www.nationalsoccerhof.com
Hall of Fame of past American soccer players

The National Football Museum, Manchester, England
www.nationalfootballmuseum.com
The world's largest soccer museum has the FIFA Museum Collection and the FA and Football League collections. The museum holds 40,000 objects, a library of 5,000 books, and a large amount of archive material and magazines.

The 2018 FIFA World Cup

In 2018, the FIFA World Cup finals took place in Russia. This was the twenty-first World Cup to be played, and the eleventh tournament to be held in a European country. As the host nation, Russia qualified automatically and were joined by 31 teams from around the world who got through via regional qualifying tournaments. Russia was knocked out by Croatia, who lost to France in the final.

National Football Museum

Glossary

A referee's uniform

AFRICA CUP OF NATIONS First staged in 1957. African national teams compete for the trophy every two years.

AGENT The person who acts on behalf of a soccer player in the arrangement of a transfer or a new contract.

ASSISTANT REFEREES Formerly known as linesmen, one covers each side of the field. They signal offside, throw-ins, fouls, and substitutions.

BALLON D'OR An annual FIFA award given to the world's best male and female soccer player.

BOOK The referee books players when they have committed an offense. They show players a yellow card and write their names in their black book. Players are sent off if they receive two yellow cards in one game.

CAP Awarded by the FA to players in an international match. Players count their international appearances in caps.

COACH Runs the training program, working closely with the manager.

COLOR The shirt, shorts, and socks a team wears. Most clubs have at least two different colors, a home uniform and an away uniform. A team uses its away uniform when there is a conflict of colors.

COPA AMÉRICA First contested in 1910. South American national teams compete for the trophy every two years.

COPA DEL REY An annual knockout cup tournament in Spain.

CORNER KICK Awarded when one of the defending team has put the ball out of play over the goal-line.

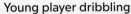

Young player dribbling

CROSS A pass made from either wing to a forward at the center of the field.

DEAD-BALL KICK A kick from nonopen play, such as a free kick or a corner kick.

DERBY A "derby match" is a game between two local rival teams.

DIRECT FREE KICK Awarded if a player kicks, trips, pushes, spits, or holds an opponent, or tackles the player rather than the ball. The free-kick taker can shoot directly at goal.

DIRECTORS The people who serve on a board to help run a club. Some put a lot of personal money into the club.

DRIBBLING Running with the ball while keeping it under close control.

EUROPEAN CUP First contested in 1956. It is now known as the Champions League.

FA CUP First contested in 1872. English league and nonleague teams compete annually for the trophy.

FIELD The field of play. In the early days, the boundaries of the field were marked by a series of flags. The FA introduced the field markings we know today in 1902.

FIFA (FÉDÉRATION INTERNATIONALE DE FOOTBALL ASSOCIATION) Formed in 1904, the world's governing body of soccer, FIFA, arbitrates between countries and runs the World Cup (Men's World Cup) and the Women's World Cup.

FOOTBALL ASSOCIATION Formed in 1863, the national governing body arbitrates between clubs and disciplines players.

FORMATION The arrangement of players on the field. The coach or manager chooses the formation and may change it during a game in response to the strengths or weaknesses of the opposition. For example, "4-4-2."

GIANT KILLER A team that beats a side believed to be of a much higher quality and from a higher division.

GLOVES Worn by goalkeepers to protect their hands and to help them grip the ball.

GOAL KICK Awarded when the ball goes out of play over the goal-line if it was last touched by the attacking team.

GPS VEST A vest worn by players with a tracking device inside for collecting performance data.

GRIP SOCKS A new type of sock with pads underneath the sole, which give players better grip inside their cleats.

GROUND STAFF The people who look after the stadium, the terraces, and the soccer field.

HANDBALL It is an offense to touch the ball with your hands or arms during play.

Ball placed on the center spot for kickoff

HEADING A defensive header sends the ball upward, clearing it as far away as possible. An attacking header sends the ball downward, hopefully into the goal.

INDIRECT FREE KICK Awarded when a team commits an offense other than a foul, such as obstruction. The player cannot score directly.

KICKOFF The kicking of the ball from the center spot to start the game.

LAWS 17 Laws of the Game approved by FIFA.

MANAGER The person who picks the team, plans tactics, motivates the players, and decides what to do in training.

MARKING Staying close to an opponent to prevent him or her from passing, shooting, or receiving the ball.

MASCOT A person, animal, or doll that is considered to bring good luck to a team.

OFFSIDE When an attacking player receives a ball, two defenders including the keeper have to be between the attacking player and the goal. Players are only penalized for being offside if they interfere with play or gain some advantage by being in that position.

ONE-TWO An attacking player passes the ball to an advanced teammate and runs on into a space. The ball is immediately returned, bypassing the defending player.

PENALTY AREA A box that stretches 18 yd (16.5 m) in front of and to either side of the goal.

PENALTY KICK A shot at goal from the penalty spot. Awarded against a team that commits an offense in its own penalty area.

PENALTY SPOT The spot 14 yd (13 m) in front of the goal. The ball is placed here to take a penalty.

PHYSIOTHERAPIST The person who helps players recover from injuries and who checks players to ensure that they are fit for a match.

A soccer card shows a player shooting.

PROGRAM Provides information for the fans about the players of their team and of the opposition, as well as a message from the manager.

RATTLE Supporters took rattles into matches until the 1960s, when they started to sing or chant instead. These rattles are now forbidden.

RED CARD The referee holds up a red card to show that a player has to leave the field. Serious foul play or two bookable offenses results in a red card.

REFEREE The person who has the authority to enforce the Laws of the Game.

SCARF Each team has a scarf in its own colors. Fans often wear the scarf or their team's color when they go to matches.

SCOUT A person employed by a club to look for talented new players.

SET-PIECE Moves practiced by a team to take advantage of a dead-ball situation.

SHIN GUARDS Pads worn inside socks to protect the lower legs.

SHOOTING A kick toward the goal.

SOCK SLEEVES Footless socks in club colors worn over grip socks.

STANDS The areas where the supporters sit around the field.

STUDS Small, rounded projections screwed into the sole of a soccer cleat. The referee or assistant referee checks all studs before play starts. Players use longer studs on a wet, muddy field.

World Cup medal

SUPERSTITIONS Many players are deeply superstitious. For example, they may insist on wearing the same shirt number throughout their career. Portuguese superstar Cristiano Ronaldo puts his right foot on the grass first when stepping onto the field.

TACKLING Stopping an opponent who has the ball and removing the ball with your feet.

TACTICS Planned actions or movements to gain an advantage over opponents.

TERRACES Steps where people stood to watch a match before the advent of all-seater stadiums.

THROW-IN A way of restarting play when the ball goes over the touchline. Awarded to the opponent of the player who last touched the ball.

UEFA EUROPA LEAGUE Originally known as the Inter City Fairs Cup, it was first contested in 1958. It changed its name to UEFA Cup and was renamed UEFA Europa League in 2009–2010.

VAR (VIDEO ASSISTANT REFEREE) A match official who reviews decisions made by the referee using video-review technology.

WARM-UP A routine of exercises to warm up all the muscles before the start of a match.

WHISTLE Used by the referee at the beginning and end of a match and to stop play when there is a foul.

WINGER A striker who plays particularly on one side of the field or the other.

WOMEN'S WORLD CUP First contested in 1991. National women's teams compete for the trophy every four years.

WORLD CUP The men's cup, first contested in 1930. National men's teams compete for the trophy every four years.

YELLOW CARD The referee holds up a yellow card to book a player.

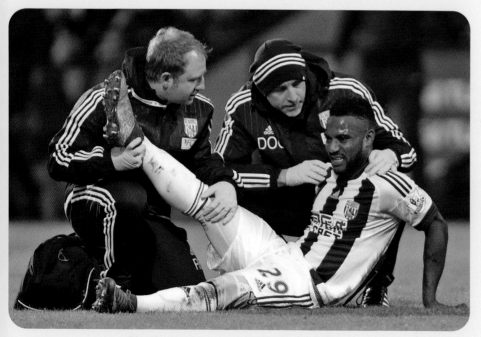

Physiotherapists treat an injured player

Index

Acknowledgments

The publisher would like to thank the following people for their help with making the book:
Hugh Hornby, Rob Pratten, Lynsey Jones, & Mark Bushell at The National Football Museum for their help and patience; Aman Kumar for editorial assistance; Diya Varma for design assistance; Neville Graham, Sue Nicholson, Susan St. Louis for the wallchart; Saloni Singh for the jacket; Hannah Wilson for proofreading; and Helen Iddles for the index.

The publisher would like to thank the following for their kind permission to reproduce their photographs:
(Key: a-above; b-below/bottom; c-center; f-far; l-left; r-right; t-top)

Action Plus: Neil Tingle 68b. **Alamy Stock Photo:** Action Foto Sport 2r, 56br, 62br; Action Plus Sports Images 35bc; Allstar Picture Library Ltd 13br, 56bl; Guy Brown 23c; Brent Clark 63cla; Dax Images 63cra; Paul Domanski 50br; Terry Foster 22–23bc; Hufton+Crow-VIEW 45crb; imageBROKER / Florian Kopp 70bl; imageBROKER / Michael Weber 56cr; Imaginechina Limited 44–45t; KGPA Ltd 8bc; Lindsay Lipscombe 69tl; MatchDay Images Limited 3cb, 61clb; Trinity Mirror / Mirrorpix 35clb; PA Images 35tr; PA Images / Joe Giddens 22–23tc, 71bl; PA Images / John Walton 52br, 61tc; picturesbyrob / fc1 69br; Eugene Sergeev 15clb; SOPA Images Limited 57crb; nath_houghton / Stockimo 45cr; Simon Dack / Telephoto Images 60tr; Nigel Waldron 63br. **Colorsport:** 68cl. **Corbis:** Chen Shaojin / Xinhua Press 17tr; Frans Lanting 65br; Matthew Ashton / AMA / Corbis Sports 34cl; Stephane Reix / Photo & Co. 34tl; Tolga Bozoglu / Epa 62l; Visionhaus 26bl. **Depositphotos Inc:** buffaloboy2513 70crb. **Dreamstime.com:** Buriy 1cb; Alexander Lebedev 12tl; Kampee Patisena 20crb; Wirestock 42–43b; Zedcreations 20crb (iPad). **Getty Images:** Adrian Dennis / AFP 43cla; AFP / Dibyangshu Sarkar / Stringer 38cb; Denis Charlet / AFP 27br; MLADEN ANTONOV / AFP 45bl; AFP / Paul Ellis / Staff 23br; Paul Ellis / AFP 59c; YANN COATSALIOU / AFP 53cla; AFP Photo / Roberto Schmidt 51ca; AFP Photo DDP / Thomas Lohnes 58cla; Allsport / Vincent Laforet 51r; David Price / Arsenal FC 61br; Bongarts / Alex Grimm / Staff 63bl; Christopher Pike / Bloomberg 65cr; Shaun Botterill / Getty Images Sport 64–65; Clive Brunskill 14bl; David Cannon / Allsport 51c; David Cannon / Getty Images Sport 64cb; Central Press / Hulton Archive 33cr; Marc Atkins 17l; Mark Cosgrove 10crb; Tom Dulat 14–15c; Berengui / vi / DeFodi Images 43tr; DisabilityImages / Trevor Williams 4bl, 25tr; Tony Duffy / Allsport 32crb; Marcelo Endrli / Stringer 38bl; Jonathan Ferrey / Staff 37br; Mike Hewitt / FIFA 2r; Stuart Franklin / Bongarts 59bc; Markus Gilliar–Pool / Bongarts 58–59c; Alex Grimm / Bongarts 35car; Richard Heathcote 49bl; Boris Horvat /

AFP 13l; Hulton Archive / Allsport / Staff / Steve Powell 33l; Seth Sanchez / Corbis / Icon Sportswire 43tl; Gerard Bedeau / Onze / Icon Sport 32cfbr; Colas Buera / Pressinphoto / Icon Sport 49crb; Catherine Ivill—AMA 29tl; Jaime Lopez / Jam Media 34–35c; Jasper Juinen / Getty Images Sport 16bl; Bradley Kanaris / Stringer 16c; Keystone / Hulton Archive 33cr, 33tl; Ross Kinnaird 58clb; Christof Koepsel / Bongarts / Stringer 10–11bc; David Leah 51cl; John Macdougall / AFP / 2005 FIFA TM 69clb; Josep Lago / AFP 57br;Harriet Lander / Copa 19r; Plumb Images / Leicester City FC 13cr; Ash Donelon / Manchester United 57t; John Peters / Manchester United 18c; Matt McNulty—Manchester City / Manchester City FC 31tr, 31crb; Clive Mason 17cr; NurPhoto 2c, 16crb; Simon Holmes / NurPhoto 39tl; Raddad Jebarah / NurPhoto 38–39b; Sergio Lopez / NurPhoto 29r; Joan Valls / Urbanandsport / NurPhoto 39cra, 58bc; Bob Thomas / Popperfoto 68cra; Popperfoto 32tr, 33crb; Popperfoto / Contributor 17crb; Power Sport Images 34bl; Gary M. Prior 62tr; Michael Regan / Staff 60b; Raul Sifuentes / Stringer 69cla; Craig Foy—SNS Group / SNS Group 42cla; Rico Brouwer / Soccrates Images 28br; Simon Stacpoole / Offside 16bc; The FA Collection / Danilo Di Giovanni—The FA 25tc; The FA Collection / Lynne Cameron—The FA 23tr; Denis Doyle—UEFA / UEFA 29cb; Michael Urban / AFP 36bl; Claudio Villa / Stringer 18bl; Visionhaus 50crb; Dave Winter 21c. **Getty Images / iStock:** LightFieldStudios 53b. **Bryan Horsnell:** 42cr **Hortweek:** 14br. **Press Association Images:** AP Photo / Lewis Whyld 45cla; Adam Davy / Empics Sport 62c; Empics Ltd 32cflb; Alastair Grant / Associated Press 71tr; PA Archive 35ca; Peter Robinson / Empics 47l; Peter Robinson / Empics Sport 57c; Witters 32clb. **Rex Shutterstock:** Dean Reid / CSM 35cla. **Shutterstock.com:** ANL 11br.

All other images © Dorling Kindersley

7cb, 7crb, 7l, 7tr, 8c, 8ca, 8ftr, 8l, 8tr, 9br, 9cr, 9crb, 9cl, 9fclb, 9l, 9tr, 10clb, 10fclb, 10tl, 10–11, 12br, 12cb (whistle), 12fclb, 13cr, 14cr, 15bl, 15ca, 16tl, 18bl, 18br, 18crb, 20bl, 20tr, 21bl, 21cra, 21crb, 21tr, 22cla, 22bl, 24ca, 24br, 24ftl, 24bl, 24tr (brass), 24tr (gauged pump), 24tr (pump), 24tr (rubber), 25cla, 25bl, 25br, 26tr, 26crb, 26br, 26cl, 27cl, 27c, 27c (hammer), 27tcr (studs), 27tr (nails), 27tr (studs), 27c, 27tr (key), 27tr (studs), 27tr (wrench), 28bl, 28tl, 29cra, 29bl, 30tl, 30br, 30cl, 30crb, 30cb, 31bc, 31clb, 31tc, 31tl, 31tr, 36bc, 36c, 36cb, 36cl, 36clb, 36cra, 36fbr, 36fcl, 36fcrb, 36ftr, 36fcrb, 36crb, 36crb (spoon), 37tl, 37tr, 37c, 37clb, 37bl, 37fbl, 37fcrb, 37fc, 38cla, 38tr, 38cl, 38br, 39cl, 40b, 40cb, 40cl, 40cb, 40cra, 41ca, 41cl, 41l, 41tl, 42tr, 43ca, 43cra, 43cra, 43fcra, 44br, 44cra, 44bl, 46bc (1986), 46bl (1978), 46bl (1982), 46br (1990), 46br (1994), 46c (1954), 46c (1958), 46cl (1938), 46cl (1950), 46clb (1930), 46clb (1934), 46cr (1962), 46fcr (1966), 46fcrb (1970), 46fcrb (1974), 46tr, 46cra, 47br, 47tr, 48bl, 48tl, 49ftl, 49tl, 49tr, 50cl, 50ca, 50tr, 51cla, 52cra, 52c, 52clb, 52fcl, 52–53, 53cra, 56tr, 57clb, 71cla; The Science Museum, London 61cblb. **Dreamstime.com:** Buriy 1cb; Alexander Lebedev 12tl;